Planet Earth

Project managed by: Tall Tree Ltd
Author: Katie Dicker
Consultant: Penny Johnson
Illustrator: Andrew Pagram (Beehive Illustration)
Designer: Jonathan Vipond
Editor: Jon Richards
Publisher: Piers Pickard
Editorial Director: Joe Fullman
Art Director: Andy Mansfield
Print Production: Nigel Longuet

Published in October 2022
by London Planet Global Ltd CRN: 554153

ISBN: 978 1 83869 522 4

Printed in Singapore
10 9 8 7 6 5 4 3 2 1

STAY IN TOUCH:
lonelyplanet.com/contact

Lonely Planet Office:
IRELAND
Digital Depot, Roe Lane (off Thomas St),
Digital Hub, Dublin 8, D08 TCV4

Lonely planet KIDS

FACTOPIA

Planet Earth

Written by
Katie Dicker

CONTENTS

WELCOME TO PLANET EARTH 6

HIGH AND LOW 8

WET AND DRY 28

HOT AND COLD 46

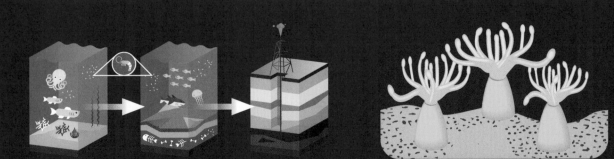

LITTLE AND LARGE.........................64

MORE OR LESS.........................86

FAST AND SLOW.........................108

GLOSSARY.........................126

INDEX.........................127

ACKNOWLEDGMENTS.........................128

WELCOME TO PLANET EARTH

This is the rocky planet we call our home —the only planet in the Solar System with the right conditions for life. It's an astonishing place. This book will show you some of the highlights.

Page 17
Earth's core

Page 11
Ocean depths

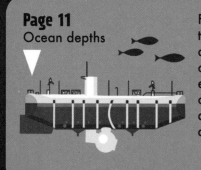

From the far reaches of the atmosphere to the deepest depths of the oceans, on this tour we'll explore some unique corners of the globe. We'll even travel down to the center of the Earth to discover its size and structure.

Page 10
Humans in space

On the following pages, we'll cross deserts, scale mountains, explore rivers, reefs, and rainforests, find out about metals and minerals, and see what and where foods are grown.

Page 21
The Death Zone

We'll marvel at scorching geysers, flowing lava, flashing lightning bolts, world-beating rainbows, and more.

Page 56
The Sahara

Page 106
Longest lightning

Page 97
Largest gold nugget

Page 107
Double rainbow

Pages 88—89
Daylight hours

Read about how Planet Earth has gradually changed during its endless journey around the Sun. We'll see how coastlines have altered, glaciers have melted, and seas have ebbed and flowed.

Page 26
Tidal bores

Page 37
Melting glaciers

Throughout this book, we'll travel to every corner of the globe, exploring its most incredible features and uncovering its most fascinating tales. So settle down for the greatest fact-filled trip of a lifetime!

Page 61
Waimangu Geyser

WHAT AN ATMOSPHERE

Earth's atmosphere extends for 6200mi —nearly as far as Earth's diameter.

The atmosphere is formed of five layers. These are, from ground level up, the troposphere, stratosphere, mesosphere, thermosphere, and exosphere.

The exosphere is by far the largest layer, reaching the depths of space from around

620 – 6200 miles.

Temperatures in the exosphere vary greatly, from a freezing 30°F to a scorching 3100°F. This layer is closest to the Sun, but the air is often too thin to absorb the heat.

The molecules in the exosphere are so far apart, you could easily fly through them without hitting any.

There's **less friction** in the thin air of the upper atmosphere. This makes it possible for satellites to stay in orbit for a long time.

It's difficult to say exactly where space begins, but many scientists use a boundary known as the Kármán Line, which is 62 miles above Earth's surface. This is the point where air becomes too thin for normal aircraft to fly.

Extent of atmosphere: 6200mi

Earth's average diameter: 7918 miles

Kármán Line: 62mi

The troposphere is about **5mi higher** near the Equator than the poles because the warmed air becomes less dense.

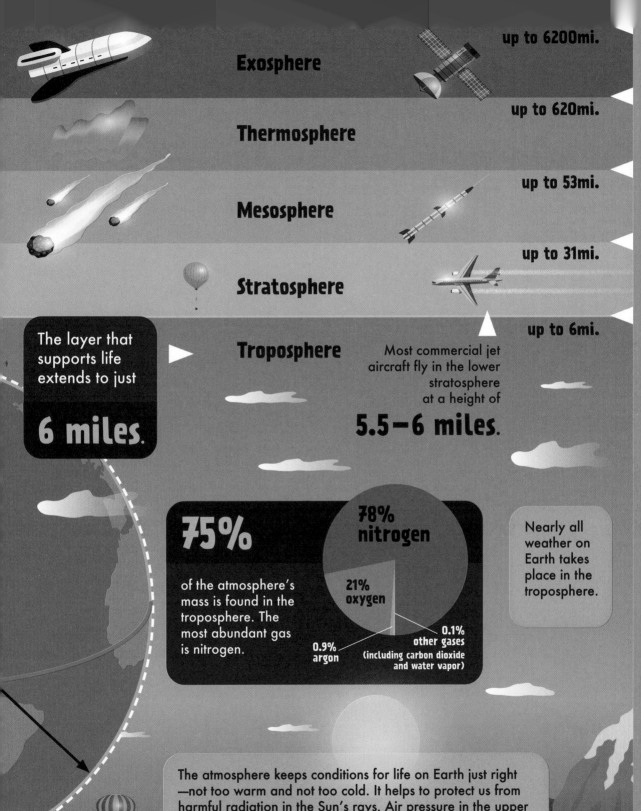

Exosphere

up to 6200mi.

Thermosphere

up to 620mi.

Mesosphere

up to 53mi.

Stratosphere

up to 31mi.

Most commercial jet aircraft fly in the lower stratosphere at a height of

5.5–6 miles.

up to 6mi.

Troposphere

The layer that supports life extends to just

6 miles.

75%

of the atmosphere's mass is found in the troposphere. The most abundant gas is nitrogen.

78% nitrogen

21% oxygen

0.9% argon

0.1% other gases (including carbon dioxide and water vapor)

Nearly all weather on Earth takes place in the troposphere.

The atmosphere keeps conditions for life on Earth just right —not too warm and not too cold. It helps to protect us from harmful radiation in the Sun's rays. Air pressure in the upper atmosphere also destroys meteoroids before they reach Earth's surface. We see these as "shooting stars."

VISITOR NUMBERS

Around **600** people have been into space... ▶

That's about **10** a year since the very first astronaut, the Russian Yuri Gagarin, went up in 1961.

◀ Around **240** people have performed spacewalks from the International Space Station (ISS). Over180 of these have been Americans.

12 people have stood on the surface of the Moon, and another **12** have flown nearby.

▼ Over **250** people have visited the International Space Station since it first started orbiting Earth in 1998.

400,000 people worked to put the first two humans on the Moon in 1969. Each Moon mission has required a huge number of support staff.

6 astronauts are normally on board the ISS at any one time.

...but only about **20** people have been to the deepest depths of the ocean.

Nobody had been at all until 1960, and there were no more trips until over 50 years later. Our atmosphere has been explored more thoroughly than our ocean depths.

In 1960, the Swiss Jacques Piccard and the American Don Walsh became the first people to explore the ocean's deepest point, the Mariana Trench, in their undersea craft, *Trieste*.

DEPTH: 35,814ft

US film director James Cameron made another descent in 2012. He traveled solo in his *Deepsea Challenger* submersible. It took two hours to reach this depth.

DEPTH: 35,787ft

Since 2019, several more people have traveled down aboard the submersible DSV *Limiting Factor*. Most trips have been captained by the American Victor Vescovo.

DEPTH: 35,853ft

2000ft

is the deepest anyone has dived using a diving suit.

Vescovo has visited the deepest point in all five oceans. He's also climbed Mount Everest, which means he's climbed and descended a combined height and depth of

64,885ft.

FIRST AMONG EQUALS

The 188 tallest mountains on Earth are all in Asia...

22,029ft

is the height of Mount Everest, the tallest mountain of all. It lies in the Himalayas on the border between China and Nepal. The first people to reach its summit were Edmund Hilary of New Zealand and Tenzing Norgay from Nepal in 1953.

22,837ft

The highest mountain outside Asia and the 189th tallest on Earth is Aconcagua in Argentina, South America.

20,310ft
Denali, USA (highest in North America)

19,341ft
Mount Kilimanjaro, Tanzania (highest in Africa)

16,050ft
Mount Vinson (highest in Antarctica)

14,793ft
Mount Wilhelm, Papua New Guinea (highest in Oceania)

2717ft
Burj Khalifa

The world's tallest building is less than a tenth the height of the world's tallest mountain.

486ft
Mount Wycheproof, Australia

Mauna Kea means **"white mountain".** In winter, it is often topped with a blanket of snow.

...but Earth's tallest peak is actually underwater.

If Mauna Kea was on land, it would be roughly the **height that airplanes fly.**

32,697ft

is the height of Mauna Kea, a volcano in Hawaii, when measured from the sea floor. If you drained all of Earth's water, it would be the world's largest peak.

From the sea floor, it is over 3600ft taller than Mount Everest.

Mauna Kea also rises

13,803ft

above sea level.

Underwater mountains can grow taller because the water helps to support their weight against the force of gravity.

Mauna Kea began to form around 1 million years ago. It is a dormant volcano that last erupted 4600 years ago. It was formed from sticky lava that doesn't flow far, but builds up into tall steep sides.

18,510ft
Mount Elbrus, Russia
(highest in Europe)

Undersea mountains, known as seamounts, are hard to find, but scientists think those measuring over 4920ft may number at least

30,000.

The smallest registered mountain in the world is Mount Wycheproof in Australia. You can walk to the summit in a few minutes.

SUN SEEKERS

The mountain peak closest to outer space isn't Mount Everest...

At 20,549ft, Mount Chimborazo in Ecuador is 8480ft shorter than Mount Everest (29,029ft), as measured from sea level.

But when you compare the two mountains, the tip of Mount Chimborazo is closer to space by over

6600ft.

3967 miles

is the distance of the summit of Mount Chimborazo from Earth's center, which is 1° south of the Equator.

...and every mountain on Earth is dwarfed by a mountain on Mars.

Mars' highest mountain, Olympus Mons, is nearly three times the height of Mount Everest at

72,000ft.

Olympus Mons is a shield volcano, which means it has a wide, gently sloping shape formed from a slow flow of lava over **billions of years.**

▲ **29,029ft**
Mount Everest

Low atmospheric pressure on Mars
means its volcanic eruptions are faster than those on Earth

3966 miles

is the distance of the summit of Mount Everest from Earth's center, which is 27° north of the Equator.

The Equator is an imaginary line running around Earth's middle, halfway between the two poles. The distance from the Equator at sea level to Earth's core is

3963 miles.

The peak of Mount Chimborazo is the farthest point from Earth's center, but measured from sea level, it's only the 39th highest mountain in South America.

Earth's diameter at the Equator is **27mi.** thicker than the pole-to-pole diameter. This is because Earth's spin causes it to bulge out slightly around the middle. This also means that gravity is slightly weaker at the Equator than at the poles.

Nearly **25** times wider than it is high, it has broad slopes and covers an area about the size of the state of Arizona, USA.

...but with **lower gravity**, the lava flows farther before it cools.

DIG DEEP

The deepest hole ever dug is deeper than the deepest part of the ocean...

The deepest naturally occurring place on Earth's surface is over two-thirds of a mile shallower than the Kola Superdeep Borehole. Challenger Deep in the Mariana Trench reaches depths of about

6.8miles.

40,230ft

is the depth of the world's deepest human-made hole. Dug in Russia from 1970, it took nearly 20 years to reach the hole's maximum depth of over 7.46 miles.

The Kola Superdeep Borehole,

as it's known, is only 9in wide and was sealed and abandoned in the 1990s.

356°F

Scientists wanted to drill deeper but they had to stop. Their equipment couldn't withstand the higher-than-expected temperatures found at these depths and the rocks became too difficult to drill through.

If Mount Everest was placed at the bottom of the Mariana Trench, there would still be over 1.24 miles of water above it. And the Kola Superdeep Borehole would tower over Mount Everest by more than

1.86mi.

2717ft
Burj
Khalifa

The world's tallest building would fit into the Kola Superdeep Borehole almost

15 times.

If you drilled a tunnel straight through the center of Earth and jumped in, it would take about 38 minutes to get to the other side of Earth!

1% of Earth's volume is the crust. The depth of Earth's crust ranges from around 3mi below the seabed to about 47 miles below some of the highest mountain ranges.

Scaled down to the size of a peach, Earth's crust would be even thinner than the peach's skin.

Earth's outer core

is made of a fluid layer of iron and nickel. It is the movement of the outer core that produces Earth's magnetism.

84% of Earth's volume is a deep layer of rock called the mantle, some of which is semi-molten.

The inner core

is right at the center of the planet. This solid, super-hot ball of metal is around **70%** the size of the Moon.

SPLASHING DOWN

The world's tallest waterfall would tower over the world's tallest building.

3212ft

is the height of Angel Falls, which was found in the depths of the Venezuelan jungle in 1937 by an American adventurer named Jimmy Angel. He was flying alone in a small plane when he spotted a giant ribbon of water tumbling over the edge of a flat-topped mountain.

Angel Falls also holds the record for the greatest uninterrupted drop of **2648ft**.

The falls are so high and so steep that the water often vaporizes into a mist before it reaches the bottom.

Four years later, Jimmy went back to explore the area. Although the falls were known to locals, Jimmy's discovery brought them to international attention. They were named Angel Falls after him. The waterfall is so remote you can only get there by airplane or boat and then a trek through the jungle

2717ft

is the height of the world's tallest building, the Burj Khalifa in Dubai, which is 495ft shorter than Angel Falls.

FREEZING UP

Some waterfalls can dry up or freeze.

Tugela Falls is found near the source of the Tugela River in the Drakensberg Mountains, South Africa. The river is usually very small here, but higher levels of snow and rainfall at certain times of the year can increase its flow. In cold conditions, the surface of the slow-moving water in the upper tiers can freeze, creating great columns of ice.

3110ft

is the height of South Africa's Tugela Falls, the world's second-tallest waterfall, which is dry for part of the year. While Angel Falls is an uninterrupted waterfall, Tugela Falls flows over **5 tiers**.

In 2015, a 263ft waterfall flowed for 24 hours at Malham Cove in Yorkshire, England, after exceptionally heavy rainfall. It was the first time a waterfall had been seen there for

200 years.

In 2019, Africa's Victoria Falls, the world's largest "curtain" of water, which lies on the border of Zambia and Zimbabwe, was reduced to a trickle after the worst drought in 100 years.

5577ft

is the width of Victoria Falls when in full flow, which is more than five oil tankers.

When in full flow, the falls create so much spray that rainbows sometimes form.

1100ft Oil tanker

19

MEASURE UP

The world's best high jumper could clear two times the average height of the Maldives.

8.04ft
high jump record

The Maldives is the world's lowest and flattest country, with an average height above sea level of

47in.

Though known as "Mount" Villingili, the country's highest point stands at just **16.7ft**.

Like other low-lying islands, the Maldives could become uninhabitable if sea levels continue to rise due to climate change.

80% of the Maldives stands less than **39in.** above sea level.

0ft sea level

Dead Sea

8382ft below sea level

is the depth of the Bentley Subglacial Trench, found beneath the Antarctic ice, the lowest point on Earth not covered by ocean.

More than **1000ft** below sea level

is the depth of the Dead Sea, between Israel and Jordan, the lowest point on land.

Antarctic ice

ANTARCTICA

Bentley Subglacial Trench

THE HIGH LIFE

If you climbed the Eiffel Tower ten times, you'd reach the average height of Bhutan.

People who live at high altitudes have adapted to the lower oxygen levels. People of the Andes, for example, have more hemoglobin in their blood to carry oxygen, while inhabitants of Tibet, China, are thought to have wider blood vessels and to take more breaths per minute.

26,240ft

is the limit at which humans can survive for any length of time. Anything above this height is known as the Death Zone because of the lack of oxygen.

The world's highest human settlement is the gold-mining town of La Rinconada in Peru, at an altitude of

16,732ft.

11,975ft

is the height of the world's highest capital city, La Paz, in Bolivia.

Bhutan in the Himalayas is the world's highest country, with an average elevation of

10,761ft.

Bhutan boasts **45** named mountains. The highest is Gangkhar Puensum, which stands at

24,836ft.

It is said to be the world's highest unclimbed peak.

984ft
Eiffel Tower

MAKING AN IMPACT

You could have stacked over **400** Big Bens into Earth's largest ever meteorite crater...

The asteroid is believed to have been at least **6 miles** wide and to have formed a crater **25 miles** deep.

◄ **315ft** Big Ben

Erosion makes its size hard to estimate, but scientists believe the crater had a diameter of about

186 miles.

Vredefort Crater in South Africa was formed when an asteroid hit Earth about **2 billion years ago.**

...but you could fit **25,000** Big Bens end to end across the largest impact crater ever known.

The crater covers nearly **1/4** of the Moon's surface.

The largest impact crater in the Solar System is the South Pole-Aitken Basin on the Moon, which measures

1550 miles wide and up to 5 mile deep.

Scientists estimate that it was formed **4 billion years ago.**

The death of the dinosaurs

was caused by the second largest asteroid impact, which created the Chicxulub Crater in Mexico. It is believed to have caused the extinction of 75% of all Earth's plant and animal species, including all the dinosaurs.

393ft

is the width of the world's most intact impact crater. Preserved by the desert climate, Meteor Crater in Arizona, USA, is about the length of 13 Big Bens laid end to end. It is relatively young, having been created

50,000 years ago.

Chicxulub Crater was up to 186mi wide and 12.4mi deep.

Located on the far side of the Moon, most of the crater can't be seen from Earth. It was only discovered in the 1960s by US spacecraft.

In 2019, China landed a spacecraft in the basin—the first time anyone had landed on the far side of the Moon.

The far side of the Moon has been found to be paler than the near side, **with more craters and a thicker crust.**

It's thought that the remains of a **giant metal meteorite** may lay buried beneath the crater's surface.

STICK 'EM UP

The world's tallest stalagmites are about 12 times as tall as a giraffe.

Son Doong ("mountain river") Cave is also the world's largest natural cave. It is over 660ft tall and 574ft wide, and has a length of

5.9mi.

The cave is about 3 million years old. It was only discovered in 1990 but was not explored until 2009.

The cave is so big, it contains a river, a rainforest, and many unique species of fish and insects. Two "skylights" let sunlight through. It is also home to a 295ft limestone wall known as the "Great Wall of Vietnam."

230ft

is the height of the two record breakers, found in Son Doong Cave, Vietnam, and Zhiin Cave, China.

Stalagmites and stalactites form when water drips from the ceiling of a cave. When the water evaporates, it leaves dissolved limestone (calcium carbonate) behind, which gradually builds up.

Stalagmites form on the floor of a cave. They can grow longer than stalactites, which hang from the ceiling, because they are thicker and have a stronger, firmer base. They tend to have rounded rather than pointed tips.

92ft

is the length of the world's longest stalactite. It's found in a cave called Gruta do Janelao in Brazil, and is almost as tall as the country's Christ the Redeemer statue.

100ft
Christ the Redeemer

Known as "Perna de Bailarina" ("the ballerina's leg"), it hangs from a 330ft-high ceiling, so in context it looks relatively small.

Like Son Doong Cave, Gruta do Janelao ("big window") has skylights that enable a small forest to grow. The cave is also home to a stretch of river.

Prehistoric paintings can be seen on the cave walls, dating back about

10,000 years.

If stalagmites and stalactites grow long enough, they may eventually meet and join together to form giant limestone pillars.

Stalagmites and stalactites grow very slowly in caves, at about
0.4in every 100 years.

GO WITH THE FLOW

There are tides that are so strong they can make a river flow backward.

The water can surge upstream at about 9mph, and the leading wave can be about 3ft high—good for rafting or surfing.

The tidal range is the height difference between high and low tide. Around the world, this is usually about 3ft.

But at the Bay of Fundy, Canada, the tidal range can be up to

39ft
—more than twice a giraffe's height.

High tide

This increase in water flow temporarily floods the Saint John River that empties into the bay, causing it to "flow backward." Known as a tidal bore, this happens twice a day.

The world's largest tidal bore is found at Qiantang River in China. Known locally as the "silver dragon," it can be up to 30ft high, reaching top speeds of 25mph.

Low tide

The tidal range in the Mediterranean Sea is about the size of a ruler.

In some parts of the Mediterranean Sea, the tidal range is just

12 inches.

8mi wide

The tidal range is so small that the Mediterranean is often called a "non-tidal" sea. Other non-tidal seas include the Baltic, the Black Sea, the Caspian Sea, and the Caribbean Sea.

The Mediterranean has an average depth of 4920ft and stretches, from east to west, for almost

2500 miles.

Mediterranean

Atlantic Ocean

Tides are caused by the gravitational pull of the Moon and Sun.

As it orbits Earth, the Moon's gravity causes the water nearest to it and on the far side of Earth

to bulge out.

▼ **These bulges are high tides.**

As the Moon continues on its orbit, the bulges subside. These are the low tides. **High and low tides happen twice a day.**

Tidal ranges are highest when the Sun and Moon are lined up, and lowest when the Sun and Moon are at right angles.

Moon's orbit

Mediterranean means

"middle of the earth."

The Mediterranean Sea is nearly landlocked —on the north by Europe, on the south by Africa, and on the east by Asia.

With its narrow inlet, the Mediterranean is also one of the saltiest seas. High temperatures mean that the sea loses three times more water through evaporation than it gains from fresh water flowing in from rivers. Water from the Atlantic Ocean can stay in the Mediterranean for

80–100 years

before returning to the Atlantic again.

22 countries border the Mediterranean, but it only has a narrow outlet and inlet with the Atlantic Ocean to the west. This maintains its low tidal range.

s e a

TAKE A RAIN CHECK

In the wettest place on Earth, enough rain fell in a year to cover a six-story building.

83.3ft

of rain, more than twice the usual amount, fell in 1985, the wettest ever year in the town of Mawsynram, India.

38.94ft

is the average level of rainfall in Mawsynram —officially the wettest town on Earth. Most falls during the monsoon season (July–October).

5000ft

Mawsynram is located high above sea level. When moist air moving from a low, flat area hits the steep hills of the region, it causes a lot of rain.

Outdoor workers wear full-body "umbrellas" made from bamboo and banana leaves which can withstand heavy rain and strong winds. They call these

"knups."

To navigate the rain-soaked valleys, locals have "trained" the roots of rubber trees to form natural living bridges. The bridges grow stronger every year, whereas man-made wooden structures would rot in the rain.

In 1966, Cyclone Denise passed over an island in the Indian Ocean called La Réunion.

During that 24-hour period, the cyclone dumped enough rain to cover the height of an adult person.

6ft

of rain fell in just

1 day

in the region of Foc-Foc, which lies

₮123ft

above sea level.

La Réunion has steep valleys and mountains which cause a lot of rain. Water in the air is forced to condense as it passes over the high ground, creating rainfall.

WET SIDE

Cyclone Denise

La Réunion has mountains in the middle. Winds bring rainfall to the eastern slopes of the mountains, while the western slopes remain dry until the hot and humid season.

DRY SIDE

Foc-Foc

New records were set again during Cyclone Gamede in 2007, when nearly 16.5ft of rain fell on the mountains over four days.

WATER YOU DOING?

The biggest hailstone ever recorded was the size of a volleyball.

← **Actual size** →

In July 2010, the community of Vivian, South Dakota, was subjected to a severe thunderstorm, with huge hailstones and winds of up to

80mph.

In the city of Villa Carlos Paz, Argentina, in 2018, huge hailstones fell that were estimated to be

6–8 inches

in diameter.

8 inches across

was the size of the record-breaking hailstone, measured after the South Dakota storm. It had a circumference of 18.6in and a mass of 1.94lbs, and made a large dent in the ground. Other hailstones with diameters of at least 6 inches were also recorded.

2.2lb

was the weight of the hailstones that fell in Bangladesh in 1986, which is about three times heavier than a can of soup.

Hailstones form in thunderclouds when water droplets are "supercooled," freeze, and begin to gather together. Winds hold the hailstones in the air until they get so heavy that they fall to the ground. Gigantic hailstones usually form in "supercell" thunderstorms, which rotate, a bit like a tornado. These hailstones are so big that scientists call them "gargantuan hail."

The biggest snowflake ever recorded was the size of a dinner plate.

Large snowflakes form when ice crystals collide and accumulate. This tends to happen when temperatures are near freezing, and the crystals melt slightly and become sticky. Snowflakes also grow larger in light winds because they are less likely to break.

Actual size

15 inches

was the width of giant snowflakes that fell at Fort Keogh, Montana, in 1887. They were also 8 inches thick.

Every snowflake has a unique shape. This is because they all form in slightly different atmospheric conditions.

0.4in.

was the width, tip to tip, of the largest ice crystal ever photographed. There must have been a lot of ice crystals in the Fort Keogh snowflakes.

The shape of an ice crystal depends on the surrounding temperature. Needle-like crystals form at 23°F, and plate-like crystals form at 5°F.

Actual size ice crystal

Ice crystals are often seen suspended in the air, twinkling in the light. This is how they get the name **"diamond dust."**

JUST DESERTS

In parts of Chile's Atacama Desert, it hasn't rained for over 400 years...

The Andes Mountains block rainfall from the east, while to the west, cold currents in the Pacific Ocean mean water rarely evaporates to form rain clouds. The only moisture comes from fog.

The Atacama Desert is the driest "hot" desert on Earth. It is often used as the setting for films based on Mars. There are areas where no rain has been recorded since records began.

64.4°F

is the Atacama Desert's average temperature. Despite being a hot desert, the Atacama is much cooler than the Sahara Desert, where average temperatures are around 129°F.

129°F

64.4°F

It is difficult for life to thrive in the Atacama, but some animals and plants can survive here, including flamingos that feed and breed on the desert's salt lakes.

One third

of our planet's land surface is now either partially or totally desert—areas where less rain falls in a year than evaporates.

Death Valley

Atacama Desert

MAP KEY:

● Hot desert

○ Cold desert

...but extreme rainfall can suddenly fill a desert with color.

0.95in. was the amount of water that fell in parts of the Atacama on March 24, 2015. It was the equivalent of 14 years of rain in a day, and was the region's heaviest rainfall for **20 years.**

March 24

The rain watered seeds that had lain dormant in the ground for years. Soon, the barren landscape was covered with **desert blooms**.

Over 200 plant species are now known to survive in these arid conditions, although they only flower for a short time. This phenomenon usually occurs every 5–7 years, but is becoming more frequent.

The hottest place on Earth—California's Death Valley—also experiences a super bloom about once a decade.

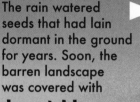

There are cold deserts as well as hot ones. An area doesn't have to be warm to be classed as a desert. It just has to receive little precipitation (rain, snow, mist, or fog)—and that makes Antarctica the world's largest desert (see page 57).

Antarctica

THINKING THE UNDRINKABLE

Less than **3%** of Earth's water is drinkable.

71% of Earth's surface is covered in water. But if this water was gathered into a single drop, it would be about 700 times smaller than Earth's volume.

97% of the world's water is found in the oceans. This water is too salty to drink.

Just 3% of Earth's water is fresh. It is found in rivers and lakes, in ice, below the ground, and in the air as water vapor.

All the water on Earth amounts to about **550 trillion** Olympic swimming pools or **333 million cubic miles**.

There's a pond in the icy Antarctic that never freezes.

ANTARCTICA

Don Juan Pond

Despite being in one of the coldest places on Earth, where temperatures can drop to –58°F, the Don Juan Pond remains liquid.

44% of the Don Juan Pond is made of dissolved salt, making it the saltiest body of water on Earth. Salt lowers the freezing point of water, which is why the pond never ices over.

69% of the world's fresh water is frozen in glaciers...

...while only about **1%** of Earth's fresh water is easily accessible.

Around 30% or,
2,000,000 cubic miles,
of Earth's fresh water is stored underground. Just 0.3% is in lakes and rivers.

Over three times that amount is stored as ice at Earth's poles, and frozen on mountains and in glaciers, amounting to roughly
7,000,000 cubic miles.

34%

of the Dead Sea is salt. This inland lake in the Middle East is 10 times saltier than the oceans. Because it has no outlet (such as a river), it becomes saltier as the water in it evaporates.

The world's oceans and seas have an average salt content of just

3.5%.

It is easy to float in the Dead Sea because our bodies are less dense than the salty water.

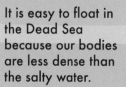

BREAKING THE ICE

The world's biggest glacier is as long as a country and moves up to 2625ft a year.

1453ft
—the height of the Empire State Building, the tallest building in the world from 1931 to 1971.

The Lambert Glacier in Antarctica is over

267mi. long, over 56mi. wide, and 8200ft deep.

You could fit about **1000** Empire State buildings along its length, about **200** along its width and nearly **six** in its depth.

Like rivers, glaciers move, although much more slowly, flowing from high land to low land. Most glaciers move about 10in a day (about 300ft a year), but some can be as slow as 20in a year.

The Lambert is the world's fastest-moving glacier, covering **1300–2600ft a year**.

The fastest glacial surge occurred in 1953 when the Kutiah Glacier in Pakistan moved over **7.5 miles in three months.**

Icebergs are smaller pieces of ice that have broken off from glaciers and drift in ocean currents.

A-76

One of the largest ever icebergs appeared in the Antarctic in 2021. Known as A-76, it was over 106 miles long and covered an area of **1660 sq miles**, making it larger than the Spanish island of Majorca.

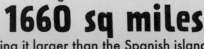
Majorca

GREENLAND

On July 31, 2019, unusually hot weather melted

26.5 billion tons

of the Greenland Ice Sheet.

The meltwater was enough to fill 10 million Olympic-sized swimming pools, or enough to cover the US state of Florida in

5.5in.
of water.

In the whole of 2019, the Greenland Ice Sheet lost

646 billion tons

of ice, adding 0.06 inches to global sea level rise (or enough to cover California in 4.1ft of water). That's more than seven Olympic-sized swimming pools a second.

Ice sheets are "continental glacier." The Greenland Ice Sheet is about three times the size of Texas, while the Antarctic Ice Sheet could cover both the United States and Mexico.

20ft

is the amount by which sea levels would rise if the whole Greenland Ice Sheet melted, which is about the height of a giraffe. If the Antarctic Ice Sheet melted, sea levels would rise about 200ft.

As sea levels rise, gravity is pulling additional water toward the Equator. This is causing Earth's waistline to spread

0.28 inches

every 10 years.

RISING DAMP

In 80 years, the ocean could be 6ft higher than it is today...

Since 1880, sea levels have risen by 9 inches, and a third of this rise has been in the last 25 years.

Sea levels are rising due to climate change. Glaciers are melting, and sea water is also expanding as it warms.

Scientists estimate that sea levels today are rising more than twice as quickly as in the past century—and they're still accelerating!

...but sea levels have been up to 66ft higher in the past.

99.7% of Earth's water is found in the oceans or in glaciers and ice caps. Sea levels depend on how much water is stored in the ice.

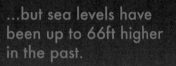

3 million years ago a period of global warming melted ice sheets in the Arctic and Antarctic. During the Pliocene Epoch, temperatures rose by up to 5.4°F.

From space, the line of an ancient shore can be seen running far inland from Florida to North Carolina in the USA. Known as the Orangeburg Scarp, it marks the extent of the sea during the Pliocene Epoch, when sea levels were 66ft higher.

Although climate change is affecting sea levels today at a quicker rate than at any time in the past...

A rise of **6.6ft** would see the Italian city of Venice submerged and parts of the UK capital, London, under water.

Every year, sea levels rise about

0.14in.

By **2100**, scientists estimate that sea levels will have risen so much that the homes of around **200 million** people will be below high tide level

—more than **70%** of whom will live in Asia.

20,000 years ago

great ice sheets buried Europe, North America, and much of Asia. Compared to today, sea levels were 400ft lower.

At this time, a land bridge connected Alaska in North America to Siberia in Asia. This enabled animals and early settlers to travel between the two continents. The land is now submerged under water.

Arctic Ocean

Land Bridge

Alaska

Siberia

Bering Sea

some of these changes are due to Earth's natural **gLacial cycle**

MAKING WAVES

The largest wave ever recorded was taller than the Petronas Towers.

In 1958 in Lituya Bay, Alaska, an earthquake triggered a huge rockslide.

The Petronas Towers in Kuala Lumpur, Malaysia, were the world's tallest buildings from 1998 to 2004.

1483ft
Petronas Towers

40 million cubic yards,

or around 3 million dump trucks, of rock plunged into the bay, forcing out the same amount of water in the form of a giant wave.

1.5 square miles

of trees and vegetation were swept away. Evidence of the catastrophe can still be seen from space.

In 2019, a 3D simulation of the wave confirmed that it reached a run-up height of

1719ft

At the time, there were three fishing boats in the bay. Amazingly, those on board two of the boats survived.

The world's most destructive tsunami moved the North Pole.

On December 26, 2004, a devastating underwater earthquake stretched over 870mi beneath the Indian Ocean and lasted

10 minutes.

The ocean floor rose by up to 130ft, almost the height of Nelson's Column in London, UK, triggering a massive tsunami. At some shorelines, waves reached run-up heights of

100ft.

The earthquake very slightly altered Earth's axis, shifting the North Pole by about

1 inch.

BANGLADESH

MYANMAR (BURMA)

INDIA

THAILAND

SOMALIA

MALDIVES

KENYA

MALAYSIA

SRI LANKA

TANZANIA

INDONESIA

SEYCHELLES

2004 Indian Ocean Earthquake

500 mph

SOUTH AFRICA

MADAGASCAR

Indian Ocean

is speed at which tsunami waves can travel in deep water, roughly the equivalent of a jet plane.

14 countries were affected and over **230,000 people** lost their lives.

DROP IN THE OCEAN

In the middle of the Pacific Ocean, the nearest humans are astronauts in space.

Covering 60 million square mi, the Pacific is the world's largest and deepest ocean. It has an average depth of 13,000ft and covers 30% of Earth's surface.

158 million cubic miles

is how much water the Pacific contains, which is over half the world's total ocean water. It holds more than twice as much as the Atlantic, the next-largest ocean.

All the world's continents could fit inside it.

The Pacific stretches from the USA to China and from the Arctic to the Southern Ocean around Antarctica.

▼

Pacific Ocean

EQUATOR

Indian Ocean

The Pacific is so large that its water temperature varies by **up to 86°F**, depending on whether you're near the poles or the Equator.

Point Nemo

The Pacific's greatest length from north to south is **9000mi.** and its greatest width is **11,000mi.**

Point Nemo is the farthest point from land. The nearest inhabited land is over 1675 miles away. It is so remote that the closest humans are on the International Space Station, 250 miles up above. No wonder Pacific means "peaceful." ▶

SEA WHAT'S HAPPENING

The world's smallest sea is about the size of the USA's largest island.

Seas are partially enclosed by land, while oceans are wide expanses.

The world's five smallest seas all cover less than **150,000 sq miles**.

149,000 sq mi.
Baltic Sea

62,000 sq mi.
Cortez Sea

93,000 sq mi.
Persian Gulf

147,000 sq mi.
Yellow Sea

The smallest sea, the Sea of Marmara, is about 174 miles long and 50m miles at its widest point, with a maximum depth of 4380ft. That makes it roughly the same size as the island of Hawaii at about

4380 sq miles.

The Sea of Marmara is an inland sea. It separates the Asian and European parts of Turkey. Marmara comes from the Greek word for "marble."

4030 sq miles
Hawaii

Sea of Marmara

TURKEY

Turkey sits on a tectonic boundary between the Eurasian Plate, the African Plate, and the Arabian Plate. Scientists believe the Sea of Marmara was formed by movements of tectonic plates around 2.5 million years ago.

STORMS BREWING

Hurricanes, typhoons, and tropical cyclones are exactly the same thing.

The only difference between them is where they occur. Hurricanes are found in the North Atlantic Ocean and the Northeast Pacific, typhoons are found in the Northwest Pacific, and cyclones are found in the South Pacific and Indian Ocean.

Tropical storms are given names when their winds reach **39mph**. And when the winds hit **74mph**, they're upgraded to hurricanes, typhoons, and tropical cyclones.

1964 was officially the world's stormiest year.

38 storms were named in the West Pacific, the highest number on record.

Of these, **26** developed into typhoons—the first, named "Tess," in May, and the last, "Opal," in December.

Each storm is given an official name. Since 1979, these have alternated between male and female names. The letters Q, U, X, Y, and Z are considered too difficult to use. If there are more than 21 storms in a year, letters of the Greek alphabet are used instead.

The center, or **"eye,"** of the hurricane is usually the safest part, as that's where the winds are slowest.

The largest ever tropical storm was almost half the size of the USA.

Typhoon Tip grew over the Pacific Ocean in 1979, with winds exceeding

186mph.

◄ The eye of the storm grew up to 9.3mi wide. This is about 50 times the length of a large cruise ship.

1367mi.

◄ was the storm's diameter, which was almost double the previous record of 700mi set by Typhoon Marge in 1951.

Eye of the storm

The storm followed a course across the West Pacific, where it eventually reached Japan. There, more than 22,000 homes were flooded and nearly 100 people died.

Military surveillance aircraft flew into the storm 40 times to collect data. ►

Most powerful storms form over the

Pacific Ocean.

IN THE EXTREME

It's so hot in Death Valley that you don't feel sweaty.

This is because the sweat on your skin evaporates immediately.

130°F

is the highest recorded temperature on Earth. It was set at Furnace Creek in Death Valley in August 2020 and July 2021.

Death Valley is the **hottest, driest,** and **lowest** place in North America.

The narrow valley has such steep sides that when the Sun warms the rocks and soil, the heat becomes trapped. In the summer, night temperatures can still be above

86°F

No rain was recorded there in 1929 and 1953, and average rainfall per year is less than

0.8 inches.

That makes Death Valley drier than the Sahara Desert.

Greater temperature extremes can be found in space.

887°F

is the temperature of Venus, the hottest planet in the Solar System. That's eight times hotter than Death Valley.

Although Mercury is closer to the Sun, Venus' atmosphere is full of carbon dioxide that traps heat. It is so hot on Venus that the metal lead would melt on its surface, as it has a melting point of 621.5°F.

In parts of Antarctica, it's so cold that it's dangerous to breathe in the air directly.

−128.6°F

is the lowest temperature ever measured on Earth. It was taken in July 1983 at Vostok Research Station, Antarctica.

Antarctica is not just the **coldest** continent, with an average altitude of 8200ft, it's also the **highest**.

At these temperatures, the air is so cold that it can seriously damage your lungs. Scientists wear masks that warm the air before they breathe it in, or breathe through snorkels built into their jackets, allowing their body to warm the air first.

The poles are so cold because sunlight falls on them at a shallower angle than at the Equator. Any energy is therefore spread out over a larger area. Temperatures are also cold because the ice reflects a large amount of sunlight, and the cold, dense air at the poles sinks, which stops clouds from forming and insulating the region.

The coldest recorded place in the Solar System is found in the permanently shadowed craters near the Moon's south pole.

−396°F

On spacewalks, conditions can be as cold as

−249°F.

Astronauts wear insulated spacesuits that have internal heating systems.

ROCK AND ROLL

Earth is constantly recycling its rock.

Like a giant jigsaw, Earth's outer surface is divided into huge rock "plates" that move slowly over the mantle beneath. When liquid magma bubbles up between (or through) the plates and cools, it forms new crust.

There are two types of plate: oceanic, which lie beneath the seas; and continental, which form the land. The oceanic plates are thinner and denser. They can slide under other plates to melt into the magma. The ocean floor is recycled about once every

200 million years.

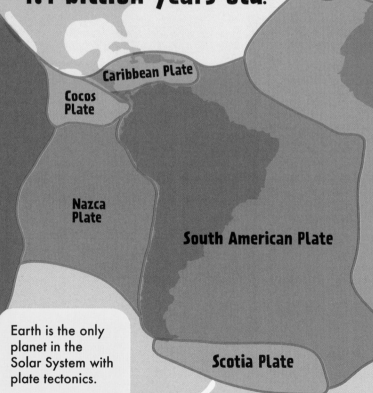

North American Plate

Continental plates are less dense than oceanic plates and can't sink into the mantle, so the rocks on land are older. The oldest rocks and minerals we've found are really ancient—almost as old as Earth at about

4.4 billion years old.

Pacific Plate

Juan de Fuca Plate

This movement of plates is known as "plate tectonics" and scientists believe it began about 3 billion years ago. It was easier for plates to break apart then because temperatures in the mantle were a whopping

2900°F.

Caribbean Plate

Cocos Plate

Nazca Plate

South American Plate

Earth is the only planet in the Solar System with plate tectonics.

Scotia Plate

Antarctic Plate

SLOWLY DOES IT

Earth's rocky plates move at the same rate that a fingernail grows.

Earth's continental plates move very slowly at about

1–2in. a year.

About 500 years ago,

people noticed that the coastlines of Africa and South America were like matching jigsaw pieces. But why had they split apart? Some thought the continents had broken up because Earth was expanding.

North American Plate

In 1912, German scientist Alfred Wegener came up with the idea that all of Earth's continents had once been a **single landmass** called Pangaea ("all lands"). Over time, these continents had moved and divided into the seven continents we know today. This became known as the theory of plate tectonics.

Eurasian Plate

Arabian Plate

Indian Plate

Philippine Plate

African Plate

Australian Plate

Pacific Plate

When Earth's oceanic plates slide and melt into the magma, they are pulled as well as pushed. This can make them move **3 times faster.**

Earth's plates collide, forming mountains; spread apart, creating new crust; and slide past each other, causing earthquakes. Whenever molten magma reaches the surface, volcanoes or new crust can form.

49

HOT SPOTS

There are four times more volcanoes underwater than on land.

Most volcanic eruptions in the oceans are found where **plates spread apart.**

Almost all of the world's active volcanoes are found at plate boundaries, the majority of which are located under the sea.

An active volcano is classified as one that's erupted in the last **10,000 years.**

Hawaiian Islands

Movement of plate

Pacific Plate

Hot spot

Most active volcanoes on land occur where **plates collide.**

But some volcanoes erupt in the middle of plates at "hot spots". The Hawaiian islands are still being formed from a hot spot in the middle of the Pacific Plate. As the Pacific Plate moves very slowly over the hot spot, a "string" of over 140 Hawaiian islands has formed.

The youngest Hawaiian island is 300,000 years old, while the oldest is 65 million years old.

0.75mi.

is the depth of the deepest volcanic eruption ever seen in the Pacific Ocean. That's nearly three times the height of the Empire State Building.

Magma and lava are the same thing. Liquid magma underground is called lava when it reaches the surface.

Underwater volcanoes are less explosive than ones on land because they have the weight of water pushing down on them.

UNDER FIRE

The Pacific Ocean is surrounded by a Ring of Fire.

RING OF FIRE

3/4

of the world's active volcanoes are found around the edge of the Pacific Plate.

25,000mi.

is the length of this ring of volcanic activity, which is about the same size as Earth's circumference.

Pacific Ocean

Over 1830°F

—that's how hot lava can get. But its super-hot outer surface cools and solidifies almost immediately when it meets cold seawater. Shallow water around it turns instantly to steam.

Some underwater volcanoes form lava "pillows"— the outer skin solidifies and stretches like a balloon as hot rock pushes outward from the inside.

In shallower water, underwater volcanoes are more explosive. They can form rivers of lava that flow across the seabed.

TAKE A DIP

Some ocean water is below 32°F but never freezes...

Temperatures across the oceans can vary by more than 54°F. The average surface temperature of ocean water is

68°F.

In the Arctic Ocean in the far north, the saltiness of the water means it can stay liquid at low temperatures. Throughout the year, surface water temperatures there can be as low as

28.4°F.

The deeper you dive, the darker and colder it gets. Cold water is denser than warm water and sinks, adding to the coldness. At a depth of 6600ft, the average temperature is

36.5°F...

...while the bottom of the ocean can be less than

33.8°F.

...but there's scalding water on the ocean floor.

In 1977, scientists noticed wide changes in ocean temperature along the mid-ocean ridge in the Pacific. Over short distances, temperatures varied from almost freezing to

750°F.

Scientists discovered **"black smokers"** —vents (openings) in the rocky seabed, out of which shoot plumes of superheated water. These vents can be as tall as the Leaning Tower of Pisa.

The warmest oceans are near the Equator. The summer Sun warms the water's surface there to more than

86°F

86°F

28.4°F

The Indian Ocean is the warmest on the planet. It doesn't connect with the Arctic, the world's coldest ocean. All year round, temperatures in the Indian Ocean are above

66°F

If seawater becomes too warm, it can't hold enough oxygen for sea creatures to survive. It can also be too acidic for sea life, and even bleach and kill coral reefs.

Warm water takes up more space than cold water, so if temperatures increase, sea levels will also rise.

Although the water reaches extreme temperatures, it doesn't "boil" and turn to steam at these depths because of the pressure of the ocean water above.

180ft
Leaning
Tower of Pisa

The plumes are formed when seawater seeps through cracks in the seafloor and is heated by hot magma below. The superheated water dissolves minerals and then re-emerges as powerful plumes of black smoky water. As the minerals cool and solidify, they form a "chimney."

INNER CIRCLE

The center of Earth is as hot as the surface of the Sun.

The inner core reaches temperatures of up to

10,800°F

Earth's core begins around **1800mi.** below the surface.

It is just over half the size of Earth's diameter, and a bit bigger than the planet Mars.

Mars' diameter: 4212mi

Mars

Earth's core diameter: 4410mi

Outer Core

Inner Core

Growing **0.04in.** a year, Earth's inner core will eventually solidify the outer core, but not for billions of years.

The outer core is mostly liquid iron and nickel, while the inner core is mainly solid iron. Although temperatures are above the melting point of iron, the inner core stays solid because of the intense pressure.

With its metal core, Earth is the densest planet in the Solar System...

Jupiter

...but the huge planet Jupiter has the greatest mass of all the planets.

Earth

It finishes its 24-hour rotation about 2/3 of a second faster—which means it laps the surface about once every **400 years**.

Earth's inner and outer core appear to rotate in opposite directions. The inner core turns eastward, like the surface, while the outer core turns very slowly westward relative to the rest of Earth.

About 500 million years

after Earth formed, it was hot enough to allow lighter, rocky material to move toward the crust and heavier metals to sink toward the center. This makes Earth older than its core.

The core moves about

100,000

times faster than the continents drift (see page 49).

Solar wind

Earth's magnetic field

Sun

Solar flare

We've never been to Earth's center, but scientists measure the seismic waves produced by earthquakes or explosions to figure out its structure.

The movement of molten metals in Earth's outer core creates a magnetic field. This protects Earth from the Sun's harmful radiation.

TOP SPOT

The Sahara is almost as big as China...

The Sahara is Earth's largest "hot" desert, and it covers

3.3 million sq miles.

Only about **25%** of the Sahara Desert is sand. The rest is mostly rock and gravel.

1063ft
Eiffel Tower

Temperatures in the Sahara can vary greatly, ranging from 122°F in the height of the summer months to 5°F among the peaks of the Tibesti Mountains.

Sand dunes in the Sahara can reach heights of over 590ft. The world's tallest sand dune is found in Argentina, and is about the same height as four Eiffel Towers—an astonishing

4035ft.

About **200 million tons**

of dust from the Sahara Desert are blown across the Atlantic Ocean every single year. Some of the dust carries nutrients that fertilize the Amazon Rainforest.

SAHARA

Mega Chad

The Sahara was once home to the biggest freshwater lake on Earth. Lake Chad is now **595 square miles**, but used to be Mega Chad, a whopping **155,000 square miles.**

...but the world's largest desert is almost 1.5 times China's size.

Antarctica is Earth's largest desert at

5.5 million sq miles.

With temperatures reaching lower than **−58°F**, the air humidity can be as low as

0.03%.

It doesn't snow very much here. When it does, the snow doesn't melt but slowly builds up to form giant ice sheets.

About 6in.

of water falls on average over the continent each year, mostly as snow.

It's so dry in Antarctica that cookies don't go stale.

On high ground, less than **2in.** of water falls as snow, while in sea areas up to 40 inches falls. However, parts of the continent haven't seen rain or snow for nearly

2 million years.

It's taken **45 million years** for ice in Antarctica to reach its current thickness.

INT-ERUPTION

There are volcanoes that have been erupting almost continuously since before World War II.

Found off the coast of southern Italy, Stromboli has been erupting since 1934 and has been regularly active since records began over

2000 years ago.

The hot lava can be seen from far away at night, giving it the nickname "Lighthouse of the Mediterranean."

Its spectacular eruptions have led scientists to describe other similar volcanoes as "Strombolian."

1933
—the year Dukono in Indonesia began erupting. It is one of the least understood volcanoes due to its remote location.

1922
—the year Santa Maria in Guatemala began erupting. Twenty years earlier, it had its first eruption for at least 500 years.

Mount Vesuvius

Stromboli

1774
—the year Mount Yasur was spotted in the South Pacific by the British explorer Captain Cook. He described it as a "great fire on an island." The volcano has been regularly active ever since.

PLAYING WITH FIRE

Deadly volcanic explosions make the surrounding land more suitable for life.

Over 270,000 people

have sadly lost their lives in the past 500 years to volcanic activity.

1 in 13 people

live within the danger zone of a volcano.

Volcanic soil formed from lava and ash is extremely fertile, making volcano slopes perfect for farmland.

Farmers tending rice paddies on the slopes of a volcano in Southeast Asia.

Volcanic regions are also rich in precious metals and minerals such as diamonds, silver, and gold.

79 CE

—the year Vesuvius in Italy erupted, completely burying nearby cities, including Pompeii, in ash and dust. Pompeii's preserved remains were only discovered in 1748.

2 million people

live in the city of Naples today, despite it being close to the active Mount Vesuvius.

Heat from underground magma is used to heat water for bathing pools and to generate electricity.

Volcanoes are also good for tourism, which brings money to a region. Every year, volcanic regions attract up to

200 million people.

RIGHT GEYSER

The most powerful geyser shoots water as high as the Statue of Liberty...

Yellowstone Park, USA, has two-thirds of all the geysers on Earth—
more than
300.

A geyser happens when water deep underground is superheated by molten rock. Eventually, it is forced up to the surface as a jet of boiling water and steam.

Steamboat Geyser can have nearly
50
major eruptions a year.

A smaller geyser at Yellowstone Park
—Old Faithful—
erupts about
20
times a day.

305ft
Statue of Liberty

The tallest active geyser in Yellowstone Park, Steamboat Geyser, can shoot water and steam over
295ft
into the air.

Old Faithful's eruptions can be predicted based on the length and height of the previous eruption. Eruptions occur every
35 minutes to 2 hours.

During an eruption, the water temperature is about
200°F
and the steam is a scorching
350°F.

300°F

200°F

... but the most powerful geyser ever shot water nearly five times as high.

Waimangu means "black water." The geyser threw black sand, mud, and rocks into the air, about once every **36 hours**.

Most of Earth's geysers occur in just five countries: the USA, Russia, Chile, New Zealand, and Iceland.

Although now dormant, between 1900 and 1904 the Waimangu Geyser in New Zealand blew material into the air up to a height of

1500ft.

200ft

is the height reached by the tallest "cold-water" geyser. Located in Germany, the Geysir Andernach erupts when cold groundwater dissolves carbon dioxide and shoots out under pressure, a bit like a bottle of fizzy soda.

Neptune

There are even geysers in other parts of the Solar System. In 1989, NASA's Voyager 2 spacecraft photographed a tall plume of nitrogen gas full of dust on Neptune's largest moon, Triton. It stretched up about

5 miles.

Triton

ALL THE RANGE

The winters in Verkhoyansk, Russia, are so cold that the ink in your pen will freeze before you start writing...

It is one of Earth's coldest places, with temperatures in winter dropping as low as

−89.9°F.

The Arctic town of Verkhoyansk is extremely remote. You can only drive there in winter when local rivers and lakes freeze over, forming ice roads. In summer, they melt, so most journeys are made by helicopter.

People run their cars all day, in case they don't start again.

Despite these challenges, more than **1000 people** live there.

The running water in the northern Russian town isn't drinkable—it's piping hot to stop it from freezing in the ice-cold temperatures. Instead, blocks of ice are taken from the river, which people store and melt for drinking water.

...but it gets hot in summer, giving Verkhoyansk the record for the world's largest temperature range—over 189°F.

In summer, the town gets a lot of sunlight:
24 hours a day.

100°F

But, unusually for somewhere so far north, temperatures in summer have risen to a baking

−89.9°F

100°F.

WELCOME
TO *Fabulous*
LAS VEGAS
NEVADA

When Verkhoyansk reached 100°F in 2020, the same temperature was recorded in the city of Las Vegas, USA, which is located in the hot Mojave Desert.

The village of Oymyakon, Russia, has also recorded winter temperatures of **−89.9°F**, with summer temperatures reaching **88.9°F**.

The Arctic is warming twice as fast as the rest of Earth. Since the 1970s, temperatures have increased by

4.1°F.

The more ice melts, the quicker the melting process gets. Ice reflects the Sun's heat, while water and soil absorb it.

DEEP SET

China's Yarlung Tsangpo canyon is three times deeper than America's Grand Canyon.

19715ft

is the depth of Yarlung Tsangpo, making it the world's deepest canyon. It's about the same height as seven stacked Burj Khalifas.

6093ft
Grand Canyon

Over 310 miles

is the length of Yarlung Tsangpo, which means it's also the world's longest canyon. It's roughly the equivalent of 5000 soccer field laid end to end.

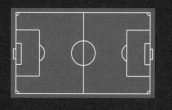

The canyon formed when Earth's plates moved and steepened the path of a river, which continued to erode the landscape.

In places, its steep valleys are full of warm, moist air from the Indian Ocean—a haven for many rare tropical plants and animals.

Temperatures in the canyon vary considerably, from

just above freezing to over 104°F.

DON'T LOOK DOWN

Canada's Mount Thor has a vertical cliff face over half a mile tall.

This granite mountain was named after Thor, the Norse god of thunder. The entire mountain stands at

5495ft.

The cliff is steeper than vertical, with an overhang of **105°** making it extremely hard to climb.

4100ft

is the height of the vertical drop of its sheer west cliff face, which would tower over the world's tallest building, the **2723ft** Burj Khalifa.

Over 30 attempts

were made to climb the summit before a four-man team succeeded in 1985. As the cliff surface crumbled, they had to avoid falling rock and ice, but the breathtaking view was worth the effort.

The climbers had to eke out their supplies. They took enough for 28 days, but the climb took

33 days.

ARCH-RIVALS

The world's longest
natural arch could
span a football field.

398ft

is the length of the Xianren
Bridge in China, the world's
longest natural arch. The
locals call it "Fairy Bridge."
Little was known about it
worldwide until 2009, when
US engineer Jay Wilbur
spotted the arch online on
Google Earth.

UNDERWORLD

Australia's Uluru is a huge rock, but what we
can see is small compared to what lies beneath.

1142ft

is the height of Uluru. It is also
2.2 miles long
and nearly
1.2 miles wide.
It takes 3.5 hours to walk
around its 5.8mi base.

456ft
Great Pyramid of Giza

Uluru isn't a giant boulder sitting
on the surface. It's more like the tip of an
iceberg. Underground, there's at least a further

1.6 miles of rock

Arches National Park in Utah has over
2000 natural arches.

Natural arches form over millions of years when a layer of soft rock is weathered and worn away beneath a layer of hard rock.

The previous record-holder for the longest arch can be found there. Known as Landscape Arch, it stretches

305ft.

Desert surface

1063ft
Eiffel Tower

305ft
Statue of Liberty

About 500 million years ago, when Uluru was starting to form, it lay in an area covered by sea. Sand fell to the bottom of the sea where, over millions of years, it was gradually turned into a layer of sandstone rock. Movement of Earth's crust then folded the rock upward. Over the past 300 million years, some of the softer rocks eroded away, revealing the shape we see today.

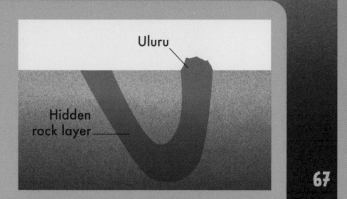

Uluru

Hidden rock layer

RIVER DEEP

The River Nile flows through 11 countries and brings deserts to life...

...but the world's largest river is in the sky.

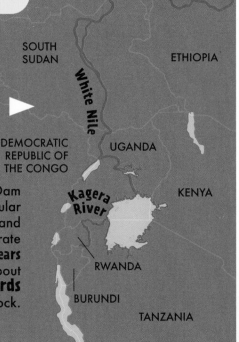

Mediterranean Sea

EGYPT

Nile

4160mi.

is the length of the world's longest river, the Nile in Africa. It stretches from Burundi to the Mediterranean Sea.

Aswan High Dam

Red Sea

SUDAN

Atbarah River

ERITREA

Floodwater from the Nile used to carry nutrient-rich soil, making the desert riverbanks perfect for farming. But the area was also prone to drought.

Blue Nile

The Nile has three main sources: the White Nile, the Blue Nile, and the Atbarah. The farthest point is the Kagera River in Burundi.

SOUTH SUDAN

ETHIOPIA

White Nile

DEMOCRATIC REPUBLIC OF THE CONGO

UGANDA

In 1970, the Aswan High Dam was built to provide a regular supply of water for homes and farms, and to help generate electricity. It took **11 years** to build the dam, with about **58 million cubic yards** of earth and rock.

Kagera River

KENYA

RWANDA

BURUNDI

TANZANIA

53 million gallons

is the amount of water that the Amazon River in South America empties into the ocean every second, making it the world's largest river by volume. It is slightly shorter than the Nile at **3977 miles**. During the rainy season, its width changes from **3 miles to 31 miles.**

The Amazon flows east toward the Atlantic Ocean. Millions of years ago, it flowed west and even in both directions, as the changing landscape raised different areas of ground.

There are three "rivers" in the Amazon Basin: the Amazon, which winds along the surface through the rainforest; the Hamza, which is a moving mass of underground water below the Amazon; and an **atmospheric river in the sky**.

Up to
5285
billion gallons

of water vapor is released each day into the sky by the rainforest. When this "atmospheric river" reaches the Andes Mountains it is blocked and redirected south as far as Argentina, where it falls as rain.

A large tree in the Amazon Rainforest can release about **264 gallons** of water a day.

In 2007, Slovenian Martin Strel swam most of the length of the Amazon River—3273mi—in 66 days.

About 2.5 miles below the surface, the Hamza "river" is as long as the Amazon River and twice as wide. This groundwater moves slowly through porous rocks

RIDGE BACK

The Andes are the longest mountain range on land...

The Andes started to form when two tectonic plates collided around **30 million years ago.**

4720mi.

is the length of the Andes range, which spans the entire length of South America's west coast and passes through seven countries.

SOUTH AMERICA

Andes

At **125–250 miles** wide, the range is around 25 times longer than it is wide.

...but the world's longest mountain range is actually found underwater.

The mid-ocean ridge is nine times the length of the Andes at nearly **40,000mi.**

Formed from the movement of Earth's tectonic plates, it runs through the Atlantic Ocean, the Pacific Ocean, and the Indian Ocean.

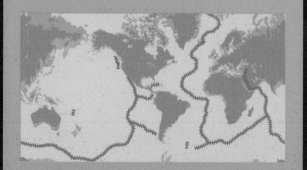

The ocean floor first began to be mapped in the 1850s. Initially, scientists used heavy cannon balls attached to cables and recorded when they reached the seabed. Later, they took more accurate readings using sound waves and their echoes.

22,615ft

is the height of Ojos del Salado, on the border between Argentina and Chile, the highest active volcano in the world.

With a wingspan of up to 11ft, the Andean condor is the world's largest flying bird. It can soar to altitudes above

16,400ft.

Although we've mapped about half of the mid-ocean ridge, the areas we've explored in detail make up **less than 1%.**

8200ft

is the average depth to the top of the mid-ocean ridge. Most of the range's peaks are far below the surface.

The ridge has gradually formed as Earth's plates have split apart. Different sections move at different speeds. Fast-moving plates have created tall, narrow mountains, while slow-moving plates have formed more gentle slopes.

OCEAN LIFE

The Great Barrier Reef is the largest living structure on the planet...

Found in the Coral Sea, off the northeast coast of Australia, the Great Barrier Reef Marine Park is bigger than Italy, covering

Great Barrier Reef

AUSTRALIA

It is found at depths of between **115ft and 6600ft.**

135,000 sq miles.

...but it is made up of billions of tiny organisms.

The Great Barrier Reef is made of corals of all shapes and sizes. Each coral is formed of polyps —tiny organisms related to sea anemones—that attach themselves to rocks. The polyps are soft but have a hard limestone skeleton at their base. These skeletons connect to form the corals, and the corals connect to form reefs.

Polyps

Skeleton

From 100,000 to 30 million years

is the time it takes for a barrier reef to fully form.

Coral reefs cover less than **1%** of the ocean floor...

It is 500,000 years old,

making the Great Barrier Reef young. Some reefs in the Pacific Ocean are up to **45 million years old.**

1453ft Empire State Building

In 2020, scientists discovered a coral reef on the northern side of the Great Barrier Reef that was taller than the Empire State building, at

1640ft.

With about **3000** individual reefs and 900 coral islands, the reef is home to a wide range of marine animals, including over 1500 species of tropical fish.

Corals grow slowly, at a rate of **0.1 to 4in a year** —about the same speed as the hair on your head. For a single reef to form, it can take up to **10,000 years.**

All the polyps in a coral colony are genetically the same. Parent polyps produce identical versions of themselves, a process known as "budding."

Coral reefs are very colorful, but coral polyps are transparent. They get their color from the algae that live within them.

180mi.

is the length of the world's second-biggest barrier reef, the Belize Reef off the coast of Central America.

...but they support about **24%** of Earth's marine creatures.

AS YOU LAKE IT

Lake Baikal in Russia is so big that it's often mistaken for a sea.

5660 cubic miles

is the volume of Lake Baikal. It holds about a fifth of the world's surface fresh water. Another fifth is carried by the Amazon River.

Baikal seals, which live nowhere else on Earth, can dive to depths of up to 1300ft.

1063ft
Eiffel Tower

Over 330 rivers flow into Lake Baikal, but only one—the Angara—flows out. In winter, the lake forms a temporary ice road up to 1.5m thick.

Its great volume is aided by the deepest depth of any lake in the world, at up to

5354ft

—about the height of five Eiffel Towers.

Its surface area is just over

12,000 sq miles.

At about 25 million years old, Lake Baikal is also **Earth's oldest lake**.

The largest lake by area, the Caspian Sea, is more than twice as big as the next three largest lakes combined, at

143,000 square miles.

31,700 sq miles
Lake Superior

26,600 sq miles
Lake Victoria

12,000 sq miles
Lake Baikal

EVER DECREASING CIRCLES

Vulcan Point Island in the Philippines was an island in a lake on an island in a lake on an island.

In 1911, a powerful eruption lowered the height of Taal Volcano, creating a small crater lake. One of the volcano's cinder cones—Vulcan Point—could be seen poking above the water, forming a small island.

Taal Volcano is the **smallest active volcano in the world**. Also known as Volcano Island, it sits within Lake Taal on the island of Luzon.

Luzon Island

Vulcan Point Island

Crater Lake

In 2020, another eruption caused Crater Lake to dry up. Unless the lake fills again, Vulcan Point is **no longer an island**.

Lake Taal

Taal Volcano (Volcano Island)

CANADA

USA

Canada is home to the largest island in a lake on an island in a lake.

Treasure Island sits in Lake Mindemoya on Manitoulin Island in Lake Huron, Ontario, Canada.

Manitoulin Island is the world's largest freshwater island at

1068 sq miles.

Manitoulin Island

Treasure Island

Lake Mindemoya

Lake Huron

UNDER COVER

The Amazon Rainforest is 23 times the size of the United Kingdom.

2.1 million sq miles

is the area covered by the Amazon. In comparison, the UK covers an area of just **93,628 sq miles.**

Amazon River

Amazon Rainforest

BRAZIL

It spans **9** countries, although nearly two-thirds of it is found in Brazil.

UK

It can take **10 minutes** for the water in a raindrop to pass through the thick rainforest canopy.

390 billion

—the number of trees in the Amazon Rainforest.

As one of the most diverse places on Earth, the rainforest is home to over **2.5 million** insect species, 40,000 plant species, 3000 fish species, 1300 bird species, and 430 mammal species.

500

indigenous tribes also have their home there. It's estimated that 50 of these have never had contact with the outside world.

The rainforest generates about 16% of the oxygen produced by Earth's plants and trees.

Only **1%** of sunlight can get through the canopy in some parts, making the forest floor dark and humid.

TRUSTY TREES

The world's oldest rainforest is around 1/4500th the size of the Amazon.

Millions of years ago, Australia was a hot and humid country with plenty of rain. Later, much of Australia's landscape became dry, but rainforests survived in the Daintree region in the country's northeast.

European settlers arrived in Daintree in the 1800s. The Daintree River was named after English geologist Richard Daintree. Now the whole area bears his name. In 2021, the rainforest was handed back to the Eastern Kuku Yalanji people, its original owners.

Daintree Rainforest

AUSTRALIA

While the Amazon Rainforest is **10 million years old**, the Daintree Rainforest in Australia is around

180 million years old.

Though much smaller than the Amazon, at about **460 sq miles**, it's still around three-quarters the size of the UK's capital, London.

The Daintree Rainforest is home to an ancient tree known locally as the Idiot Fruit (or Green Dinosaur). It has a single poisonous seed about the size of a human fist.

COAST TO COAST

Canada's coastline could stretch five times around the world.

125,567mi.

is the length of Canada's coastline, the longest of any country. If you walked for **12.5 miles** a day, you wouldn't finish walking round the coastline for over **27 years.**

Canada borders three oceans: the Pacific, the Atlantic, and the Arctic. It is the second-largest country in the world, after Russia.

Arctic

Pacific

Atlantic

CANADA

Earth's circumference is approximately **25,500mi.**

FRANCE

MONACO

Mediterranean

It would take under an hour to walk around Monaco, the country with the shortest coastline, at just over **2.5 miles**

World's longest coastlines:

36,122 miles Norway

61,567 miles Indonesia

125,567 miles Canada

The border of Bosnia and Herzegovina is 956 miles long, but just 12.4 miles is coastline. That's the smallest ratio of any country at just

1:77.

OUTWARD BOUND

The Sargasso Sea is a sea without shores.

The Sargasso Sea is found in the North Atlantic Ocean, covering an area of about

1.9 million square miles.

NORTH AMERICA

Sargasso Sea

Four strong ocean currents travel in a clockwise motion, forming the borders of the sea. The Sargasso Sea drifts with the moving currents, and is about 680mi. wide and 2000mi. long.

Atlantic Ocean

AFRICA

36%

of the Sargasso Sea is salt, which is around 10 times the amount of salt in normal ocean water.

The sea is named after the dense sargassum seaweed which covers its surface, held in place by the circling currents.

SOUTH AMERICA

In 1492, Christopher Columbus crossed the Sargasso Sea and thought the presence of seaweed meant he was nearing land. He still had thousands of miles left to travel.

CHANGING PLACES

The Pacific Ocean is shrinking, but the Atlantic is expanding.

P a c i f i c

The movement of Earth's tectonic plates is causing the Pacific to shrink every year by about

1 inch.

Subduction zones

Around the edge of the Pacific, the tectonic plates are sinking into subduction zones —areas where one plate is being pushed down beneath another one. The continents are being pulled together, and some scientists think the Pacific may disappear.

Earth's continents are always moving. Scientists think the continents could eventually come together to form a new supercontinent...

RISE AND FALL

Scotland and Scandinavia are rising, while Mexico City is sinking.

20,000 years ago, during the last ice age, large parts of Earth's surface were covered in ice. The weight made the land sink down—in some places by up to **1000ft**.

SCOTLAND   DENMARK   NORWAY   SWEDEN

When the ice melted and the weight was released, the land beneath began to rise up while the land around it slowly sank back down.

ICELAND

Atlantic

In the center of the Atlantic, tectonic plates are being pulled apart at an area called the Mid-Atlantic Ridge. As the plates spread, the Atlantic is growing every year by about

2in.

Earth's plates are causing countries to grow too. Iceland sits on the northern end of the Mid-Atlantic Ridge. The pulling apart of the plates is causing it to grow by about **0.8in. a year.**

Mid-Atlantic Ridge

...but not for hundreds of millions of years.

Even today, this process is still causing the east coast of North America to sink, while Scotland and Scandinavia are rising every year by up to

0.4in.

Mexico City is sinking about 20in a year and has already sunk by

30ft.

This is because the land below the city has been drained of water. The drier, emptier ground is being compacted down by heavy buildings. Scientists think that over the next 150 years, it could sink another

100ft.

ISLE CHECK

Greenland is the world's largest island that's not a continent.

850,000 sq miles

is the area of Greenland, making it more than double the size of the second-largest island, New Guinea.

GREENLAND

NEW GUINEA

Over 1000 years ago,

Greenland was settled by colonists from Iceland. It was later inhabited by Inuit people and settlers from Denmark. The country officially became part of Denmark in 1953, although it is largely self-governing.

80%

is the amount of Greenland's surface that is covered by an ice sheet.

AUSTRALIA

At 3 million sq miles,

Australia is nearly four times bigger than Greenland, but it's classed as a continent, not an island.

Continents are usually defined as occupying their own tectonic plate. Australia lies on the Australian Plate, while Greenland forms part of the North American Plate, along with Canada and the USA.

TINY NATION

The smallest island nation is also the world's least visited country.

Pacific

Equator

Nauru lies in the Pacific Ocean, over 185mi from its nearest neighbor. Jagged coral reefs surround the island, making it difficult to reach by boat.

8.1 sq miles

is the area of Nauru, making it bigger than just two other countries, Monaco and Vatican City. But those two smaller nations lie on the mainland of Europe, and are also their own capital city. Nauru is an island without any cities.

Pacific

200 visitors, on average, make it here each year, all by plane.

NAURU

Less than 11,000

people currently live in Nauru. The government offices are located in a small district on the shore called Yaren, which is home to 700 people.

Yaren

Nauru was once the world's richest country per person.

For a short time in the 1960s, the mining of phosphate—a valuable chemical derived from bird poo—made the country very rich. Unfortunately, the phosphate has been used up and many people there now live in poverty.

Nauru's flag was designed with a line and a star to show its location next to the Equator.

POPULAR PLACES

Over half of Earth's people live in Asia, the world's largest continent.

Asia is made up of 48 countries, taking up around 17 million square miles which is

1/3 Earth's land.

Asia's largest country by area is Russia, at **6.6 million sq miles.**

More than 2300 languages are spoken in Asia, but over half speak Mandarin Chinese.

官话

RUSSIA

CHINA

Its largest country by population is China, with around **1.4 billion people.**

Asia has nearly 3.5 times the population of Africa, the second-most populated continent with **1.3 billion.**

Together, Asia and Africa share over **3/4** of the world's population.

Almost **60%** of the world's people live in Asia —that's over

4.6 billion people.

Percentage of the world's population

59.8%
Asia

16.7%
Africa

9.8%
Europe

7.6%
North America

5.6%
South America

0.5%
Oceania

WIDE OPEN SPACES

The smallest continent, Australia, has just **0.33%** of the world's population.

Australia is almost the size of the United States. From east to west, it's about

2500mi. wide.

Because the interior is so hot and dry, more than

80% of people live near the coast.

Over **85%** live in cities, such as Sydney, with its famous opera house and harbor bridge.

26 million

people live in Australia, but this population is spread out over 3 million square mi, meaning the continent has less then

9 people per square mile.

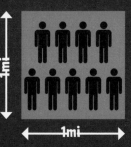

1mi

1mi

Australia is often grouped with other islands of the Pacific Ocean in a region called Oceania that is made up of 14 countries.

Pacific

Oceania

AUSTRALIA

The region accounts for about a fifth of Earth's surface, but it's mostly sea.

Over 38 million sq miles

—Oceania's total area, but only **3.3 million sq miles** of this is land.

JUST LAKE THAT

Canada has more lakes than the rest of the world combined.

900,000

lakes are dotted across Canada—over **4 times more than any other country.**

In total, there are **117 million** lakes across the world. Put together, these lakes have a surface area of **2 million square miles** —enough to cover half of Canada.

If you added the shorelines together, they would stretch about **4.4 million mi.** or around 175 times the circumference of Earth. This is **4 times longer than the world's ocean coastline.**

3.8 million square miles —the area of Canada

If all the water from Earth's lakes was spread over Earth's land, it would form a layer **4.3ft deep.**

The largest freshwater lake by surface area is Lake Superior in Canada, at over **31,500 sq miles.**

Lake Superior

USA

THIRSTY WORK

Malta has no permanent rivers, streams, or lakes.

The island of Malta is surrounded by sea, but there is no fresh water on its surface.

23.6 inches

is the amount of rainfall Malta receives a year. Much of this evaporates in the heat, meaning Malta only has about half the water it needs to support its population.

Malta extracts natural groundwater from deep below the surface, which provides up to

30 million cubic yards

of water a year, the equivalent of about

9000

Olympic swimming pools.

3270 cubic yards —the size of an Olympic swimming pool

Since 1982, Malta has also had desalination plants which remove the salt from seawater, making it safe to drink.

The world's three most water-stressed countries are Qatar, Israel, and Lebanon. By using up to 80% of their surface water and groundwater each year, these countries are at risk if weather patterns change.

80%

MIDNIGHT SUN

In winter, parts of Iceland get just four to five hours of daylight...

ICELAND

Sun

December 21

Earth's northern hemisphere tilts away from the Sun between September and April, shortening the days. Iceland's shortest day is around December 21.

The farther north you go in winter, the less daylight hours there are. At the North Pole, the Sun doesn't fully rise for six months of the year. Although twilight gives a little daylight for some weeks, the North Pole is in complete darkness for about 11 weeks a year.

Between December 21 and June 21, Iceland's daylight hours increase by

1-3

minutes a day.

For about two months of the year, you can't see the Sun in Ísafjörður, a town in northern Iceland. The Sun is so low that its rays are blocked by the tall mountains surrounding the town. ▶

Around March 21 and September 21, there's about an equal amount of daylight and darkness in both the northern and southern hemispheres. These are called the equinoxes.

Daylight hours vary greatly on other planets. On Jupiter, a day is less than half an Earth day, while on Venus it lasts for 243 days, or 5832 hours.

Mercury
58.5 days

Venus
243 days

Mars
25 hours

...while during summer in Iceland, the Sun never sets.

ICELAND

Earth's orbit

Iceland gets 24 hours of daylight around June 21, when the northern hemisphere is tilting toward the Sun. We call this the "Midnight Sun."

June
21

During the Midnight Sun, the Sun sets just after midnight and rises before 3am, but the sky doesn't go completely dark.

The Midnight Sun occurs during summer months in countries and regions north of the Arctic Circle and south of the Antarctic Circle. These include Antarctica, Iceland, Greenland, and northern parts of Norway, Sweden, Finland, Alaska, Canada, and Russia.

Between June 21 and December 21, Iceland's daylight hours decrease by

1-3
minutes a day.

Jupiter

Saturn

Uranus

Neptune

10 hours   **11 hours**   **17 hours**   **16 hours**

IN SEASON

Some countries don't have summer or winter...

Because countries near the Equator are tilted toward the Sun all year round, their days have a constant **12 hours of daylight and 12 hours of darkness.**

Although they are warm all year round, countries near the Equator have a "wet" and "dry" season. They experience high rainfall of at least **79in a year.**

79–82°F

is the average temperature of countries close to the Equator all year round.

...while other countries have six seasons.

Seasons are based on **weather patterns** as well as temperature.

Some countries, such as India and Bangladesh, have spring, summer, autumn, and winter, but also mark a rainy season and a "late autumn" season. Each season lasts for about two months. Other countries, such as Thailand, have three seasons—a hot pre-rainy season, a rainy season, and then a cool dry season.

Mount Kilimanjaro in Tanzania is just 205 miles south of the Equator, but its height means it has a cool, dry climate. It is topped by an ice cap up to

130ft thick.

Just 5.4°F

is the difference between the hottest and coldest months in countries close to the Equator.

19,341ft —the height of Mount Kilimanjaro

The North and South Poles have just two seasons: summer and winter.

Some long countries, such as Sweden and Chile, can experience different seasons at the same time. In autumn, Sweden can have warm temperatures in the south but freezing cold temperatures in the north.

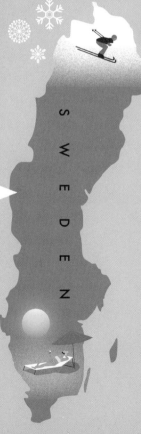

S W E D E N

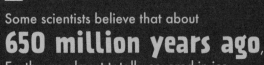

"Snowball Earth"

Some scientists believe that about

650 million years ago,

Earth was almost totally covered in ice for around 20 million years. They call this period of permanent winter "Snowball Earth."

METAL WORK

Nearly a third of planet Earth is made of iron.

Iron is Earth's most common element, making up around **32%** of the planet's mass. ▶

This is followed closely by oxygen, which makes up another **30%**.

▼

About two-thirds of the naturally occurring elements on Earth have metallic properties.

30% oxygen

O₂

32% iron

15% silicon

14% magnesium

3% sulfur

2% nickel

1.5% calcium

1.4% aluminum

1.1% other elements

Iron makes up most of Earth's core—over 80%. No wonder Earth is so heavy, weighing 13.3 septillion lb, or

13,300,000,000,000,000,000,000,000lb.

When Earth formed, most of the iron sank to its center. Nearly half of Earth's crust (47%) is oxygen, nearly a third (28%) is silicon (a semi-metal used for computer chips), and nearly a tenth (8%) is aluminum, the most common pure metal in Earth's crust.

IT'S ELEMENTAL

Everyone on Earth is
made of stardust.

The heaviest
elements were
formed from
exploding
stars called
supernovas. ▶

Hydrogen and helium
were the first elements to
form in the universe. All the
other naturally occurring
elements on Earth were
made from stars that died
millions of years ago.

Some elements,
such as berkelium,
can only be artificially produced.

Just 0.035oz of berkelium
has been created in laboratories.

Only about 0.8oz of the rarest
element, astatine, can be found
in Earth's crust at any one time.

Astatine is highly radioactive. If you had a piece
that was large enough to see, its radioactivity would
cause it to rapidly decay. In its most stable form,
half of an astatine sample decays every eight hours,
until all of it has changed into another element.
Although the existence of astatine was predicted in
the 1800s, it wasn't discovered until 1940.

Astatine atom

RUNNING LOW

As far as we know, we have just 47 years of oil left.

Oil is used to produce electricity, heat buildings and power vehicles.

97 million

is the number of barrels of oil used around the world every single day. That's about **5 barrels per person per year.**

The world's first commercial oil well was drilled in America in 1859. Since 1870, we've used at least

135 billion
barrels of oil.

300 billion

is the number of barrels of oil held by Venezuela, the most oil reserves of any country, followed closely by Saudi Arabia.

Oil began to form 300–400 million years ago when tiny sea plants and animals died and were buried by layers of sand and silt on the ocean floor. Over millions of years, enormous pressure turned the remains into oil.

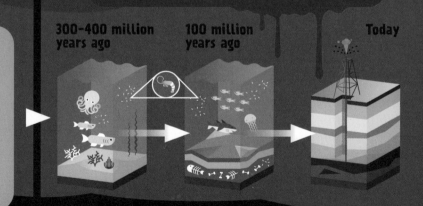

300–400 million years ago

100 million years ago

Today

We still have more than **1.4 trillion** barrels of oil we know we can extract, although there may be more resources we've yet to discover. At the rate we're currently consuming oil, we have less than 50 years of oil left, although demand is likely to fall. The development of "green energy" will help to reduce our dependency on oil.

MINE-CRAFT

Aluminum used to be more valuable than gold.

As the most common metal in Earth's crust, aluminum is now one of the cheapest metals to buy. But it can only be found in nature combined with other elements in ores such as bauxite.

Bauxite → Aluminum

1821

—bauxite was discovered.

Bauxite can be extracted from mines near Earth's surface.

1845

—a way of extracting aluminum from bauxite was invented, but it was difficult and expensive. For decades, aluminum remained rare and valuable.

1880s

—a new method for extracting aluminum was devised. It involved passing electricity through dissolved aluminum ore. Now aluminum could be produced in large quantities, and its price quickly fell.

In 1884, the USA's Washington Monument was fitted with an aluminum cap as a lightning conductor, and to show off the country's wealth. It was then the world's largest piece of aluminum, with a mass of over 4.4lb, and hugely expensive. But its value soon plummeted as the metal became more common.

In the 1850s Napoleon III, the Emperor of France, had a set of aluminum cutlery made for use by special guests.

RICH PICKINGS

All the gold that's ever been mined would fill less than four Olympic-sized swimming pools...

This gold would make a cube measuring just

69ft on each side.

Three countries have produced most of this gold: **China, Australia, and South Africa.**

...but the oceans hold about **22 million tons** of gold.

$1000 trillion

is the estimated value of the gold held in the oceans.

In 1872, British chemist Edward Sonstadt discovered gold in seawater. Since that time there have been many attempts to find a way to extract it, but none have been successful.

Gold has been regarded as precious since ancient times. About 220,000 tons of gold have been mined, around two-thirds of this since 1950. Some of the gold circulating today could have been mined thousands of years ago.

3300 tons

is the amount of gold that's now mined each year, although scientists say there may be less than 61,000 tons left to discover in Earth's crust.

159lb

was the weight of the biggest nugget of pure gold ever found. It was discovered in Australia in 1869 and was **24in. long.**

3.4 billionths of a gram

is the average weight of gold in a gallon of seawater. This means that you'd need to filter

3.4 billion gallons

to get just 1 gram—that's enough water to fill the Royal Albert Hall, London, UK, 150 times.

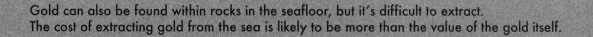

Gold can also be found within rocks in the seafloor, but it's difficult to extract. The cost of extracting gold from the sea is likely to be more than the value of the gold itself.

FOOD FOR THOUGHT

Together, India and the USA have over a fifth of the world's arable land...

10%

of Earth's land is currently farmed to grow food.

The five biggest food-producing countries are China, India, the USA, Brazil, and Russia.

...while Greenland isn't so green.

Much of the land in Greenland is covered with ice and snow, making it difficult to farm. Greenland's primary food industry is fishing.

Greenland and Suriname are the countries with the least arable land, so they rely on food imported from other countries.

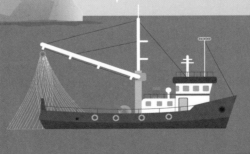

982 CE

—the year Greenland was discovered by the Viking Erik the **Red**. He named the country "**green**" to attract more settlers.

Russia is the biggest country in the world, but its harsh climate makes farming difficult in some areas. The USA is the biggest exporter of food. India and China have the largest populations, so they tend to eat more food than they export.

75%
of the world's food comes from just 12 plants and 5 animals.

The top five plants are rice, wheat, sugarcane, maize (corn), and potatoes...

40%
of the food that's grown and produced in the USA is thrown away uneaten.

...and the animals are cows, goats, sheep, pigs, and chickens.

About
800,000 years ago,
scientists believe Greenland was greener than it is now. Ice samples suggest the island was warmer during the last ice age than originally thought, and covered in forests.

In Suriname, in South America, bauxite mining for aluminum (see page 95) is a major industry, accounting for

70%
of exports.

SURINAME

Less than 1% of its land is used for farming.

GROWING PAINS

There are more people living in the USA now than there were in the whole world in 1000 CE...

7.8 billion

North America

592 million

491 million

The world's population saw the fastest growth between 1950 and 1987, when it doubled in just over a generation, from **2.5 billion to 5 billion.**

By 2100, Latin America and the Caribbean are expected to have the oldest population, with an average age of 49 (up from 20 in 1950).

4.3 billion

1.3 billion **Africa**

South America

680 million

430 million

3 billion

is the amount by which the world's population could increase this century. This rise is caused by better living conditions and healthier nutrition.

In 2100, half the world's babies are expected to be born in Africa. There, families have an average of 4.7 children, compared to the global average of 2.5. Africa's population is expected to double by 2050, and double again by 2100.

Since 1950, the world's population has grown by about 1–2% every year.

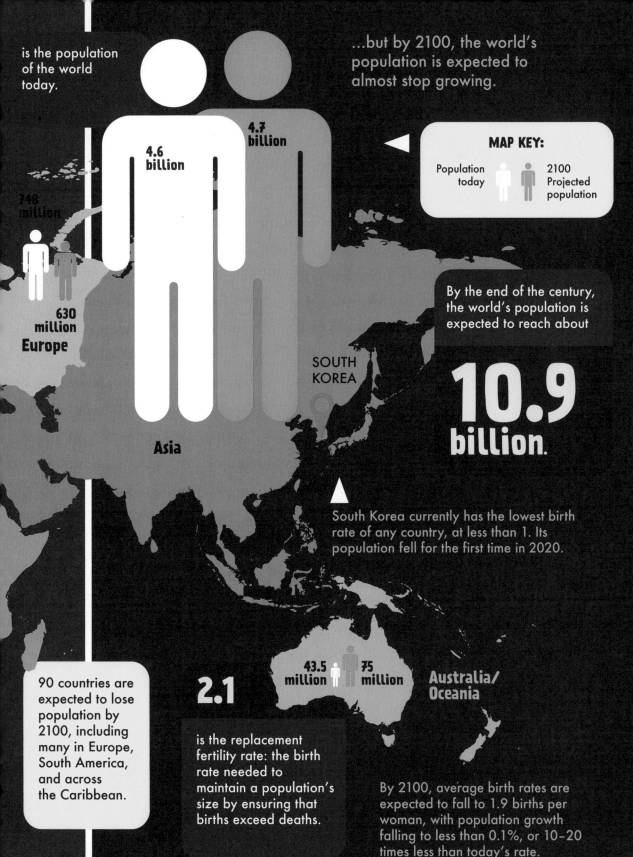

is the population of the world today.

...but by 2100, the world's population is expected to almost stop growing.

4.6 billion

4.7 billion

MAP KEY:

Population today

2100 Projected population

748 million

630 million
Europe

Asia

SOUTH KOREA

By the end of the century, the world's population is expected to reach about

10.9 billion.

South Korea currently has the lowest birth rate of any country, at less than 1. Its population fell for the first time in 2020.

90 countries are expected to lose population by 2100, including many in Europe, South America, and across the Caribbean.

2.1

43.5 million

75 million

Australia/ Oceania

is the replacement fertility rate: the birth rate needed to maintain a population's size by ensuring that births exceed deaths.

By 2100, average birth rates are expected to fall to 1.9 births per woman, with population growth falling to less than 0.1%, or 10–20 times less than today's rate.

LIVING SPACE

Asia is the most densely populated continent in the world...

388

—the number of people per square mile living in Asia today. In contrast, the global average population density per square mile is **65 people**.

Asia has the world's two most populated countries—China and India. India is expected to overtake China in around 2027.

India has a population of
1.39 billion
compared to China's
1.44 billion,
but birth rates in India are rising while those in China are falling.

Some small urban regions in Asia, such as Macao, Singapore and Hong Kong, are particularly densely populated. Macao has

56,061 people
per square mile.

▼

3243
people per square mile

is the population density of Bangladesh, the most crowded of the larger Asian countries. Its population is three times as dense as neighboring India.

PEOPLE POWER

...but that population is not spread evenly.

MONGOLIA

▶

C H I N A

While the area of Mongolia is only about 1/6 of the size of China, its population density is about 1/75 of China. It's one of the world's least densely populated countries, with

Mongolia's population of
3.3 million
is about 400 times smaller than neighboring China's.

about 5 people per sq mile.

90% of Mongolia's land is pasture or desert. The Gobi Desert covers almost a third of the country. As well as enduring droughts, Mongolia has harsh winter temperatures.

Over **25%** of Mongolia's people live as nomads. Many keep herds of animals, moving with the seasons to find fresh pasture and water, and living in circular tents called gers.

▼

But young people are moving to the cities. The population of the capital, Ulaanbaatar, has increased by 50% in 10 years, now totaling 1.6 million people.

CITY SIGHTS

Japan's capital city has nearly as many inhabitants as the whole of Canada.

Tokyo is the world's most populated city, after Delhi (India) and Shanghai (China). It's often called a "megacity."

37 million

is the population of the greater Tokyo area. The capital city has a quarter of Japan's population.

2 out of 5 people were not born in Tokyo...

SMALL ROLE

Palau's capital city has less than **250 residents.**

Pacific

It's made up of over 340 coral and volcanic islands, of which nine are inhabited.

In 2006, Ngerulmud replaced the larger Koror City as Palau's capital.

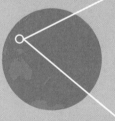

Palau is an island nation in the Pacific Ocean.

PALAU

Ngerulmud

Jellyfish Lake

Palau used to be part of the United States but gained independence in 1994.

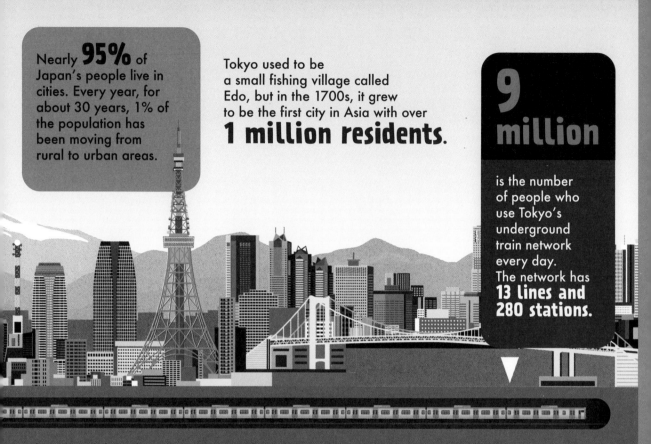

Nearly **95%** of Japan's people live in cities. Every year, for about 30 years, 1% of the population has been moving from rural to urban areas.

Tokyo used to be a small fishing village called Edo, but in the 1700s, it grew to be the first city in Asia with over **1 million residents**.

9 million is the number of people who use Tokyo's underground train network every day. The network has **13 lines and 280 stations**.

...but moved there for education, entertainment, and job opportunities.

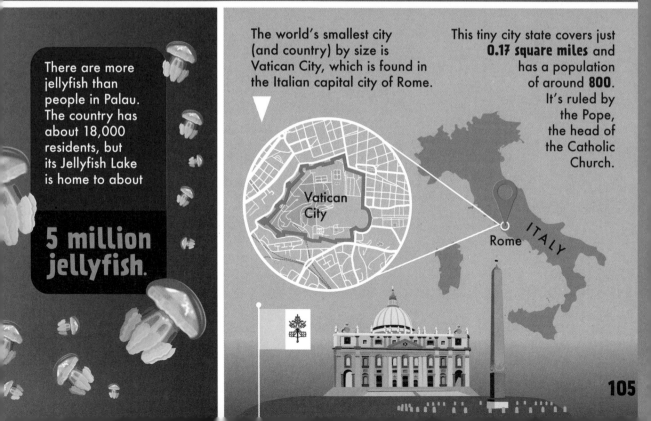

There are more jellyfish than people in Palau. The country has about 18,000 residents, but its Jellyfish Lake is home to about

5 million jellyfish.

The world's smallest city (and country) by size is Vatican City, which is found in the Italian capital city of Rome.

This tiny city state covers just **0.17 square miles** and has a population of around **800**. It's ruled by the Pope, the head of the Catholic Church.

Vatican City

Rome

ITALY

QUICK AS A FLASH

There are about **100** lightning flashes on Earth every second.

15,000

is the number of lightning strikes a night above Lake Maracaibo on the north coast Venezuela. That's 28 lightning strikes a mi

nearly one every 2 second

Known as Catatumbo lightning, the lightning over Maracaibo is caused by winds blowing across the lake and surrounding mountains, which unsettles the air, creating an electrical charge.

Used in the past b as a way o their loca dazzling lig can be se

25

a

▲ Cloud-to-ground lightning travels down, but when a connection is made with the ground, the flash you see is actually going up.

Light sky i worl reco lightn span

47

54,000°F

is the temperature of a single stroke of lightning, which can momentarily heat the air to around **5 times hotter than the surface of the Sun.**

2020 also saw the longest single lightning flash, seen above Uruguay and Argentina, lasting **17.1 seconds.**

FLYING COLORS

The longest-lasting rainbow shone for nearly **9 hours**.

Up to four rainbows were seen for a short time. Double rainbows are caused when light is reflected twice from each raindrop. The second rainbow is fainter and its colors are reversed. Very rarely, when light is reflected even more times from each raindrop, four rainbows can be seen.

The rainbow over Yangmingshan, Taiwan, in 2017 could be seen from a nearby university campus.

Water vapor had accumulated in the air, unmoved by light winds. The angle of the rainbow changed as the Sun moved across the sky, but it was still visible from various parts of the campus.

You can't get to the end of a rainbow, but you can sometimes see circular rainbows from an aircraft.

Rainbows occur on Earth because its atmosphere has suitable amounts of water vapor. Rainbows have also been spotted on Venus.

MOUNT UP

Nanga Parbat could one day overtake Mount Everest as the world's tallest mountain.

As part of the Himalayas in Pakistan, Nanga Parbat is currently the world's ninth-highest mountain at

26,660ft.

0.3 in. ↑

is the height it gains every year, making it the world's fastest-growing mountain.

Nanga Parbat means "naked mountain"—some of its sides are too steep for snow to cover them and are just bare rock.

PULL DOWN

There's a limit to how high any mountain can grow on Earth.

Earth's top 10 tallest mountains are all of a similar height, at

26,250–29,029ft.

Rivers can make mountains seem taller by eroding rock near the mountain's base. But if this causes a landslide, it can reduce the mountain's height.

Mount Everest, meanwhile, is only growing by around **0.16 inches a year.** This means Nanga Parbat could possibly overtake Everest in about **241,000 years.**

29,029ft
Mount Everest

The Himalayas were formed when the Indian tectonic plate collided with the Eurasian Plate around 50 million years ago, gradually pushing the rocks up into giant mountains.

Eurasian Plate

Today

Himalayas

INDIA

10 million years ago

38 million years ago

55 million years ago

Indian Plate

71 million years ago

Mountains keep growing until their weight makes it too hard for them to stand against the downward force of gravity. As they get heavier, their base also starts to sink into Earth's hot mantle, reducing their height. Nanga Parbat is unlikely to grow significantly taller than Mount Everest because the force of gravity will hold it back.

Mountains can grow taller on other planets because the force of gravity is weaker there. They can reach **33,000–66,000ft** tall, with Mars' Olympus Mons (see pages 14–15) the tallest of all at 82,000ft.

GONE WITH THE WIND

On the coast of Antarctica, the wind travels as fast—and is as cold—as a snowball...

The Antarctic ice sheet is dome-shaped, causing winds to blow downhill from the center to the ocean. Gravity pulls on this cold air, making it move faster—and feel even colder. These are known as **katabatic winds.**

155mph

is the speed that winds can reach in Commonwealth Bay, Antarctica, the windiest place on Earth.

The windy conditions can cause sudden whirlwinds of snow.

The wind is also teeth-chatteringly cold, averaging around

-22°F.

Despite these extreme conditions, Commonwealth Bay is a popular home for penguin colonies, which have adapted to survive in the cold and windy climate.

In 1805, an Irish naval officer named Francis Beaufort developed the **Beaufort Scale,** a visual guide to help sailors estimate the wind. It went from 0 to 12.

0
The sea's surface is like a mirror and smoke rises vertically.

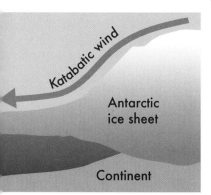

Katabatic wind

Antarctic ice sheet

Continent

...but the winds at the center of Antarctica are among the **calmest on Earth.**

6mph

is the average wind speed at the top of the Antarctic dome, in the middle of the continent. The winds pick up pace as they descend towards the coast.

Wind is the air moving from areas of high pressure to areas of low pressure. The greater the pressure difference, the quicker the air moves.

Instruments called anemometers are used to measure the speed, direction, and strength of the wind. The earliest anemometers used spinning cups to measure wind speed. Modern anemometers use sound waves and laser technology.

6
Trees bend, smoke is nearly horizontal, and waves form.

12
It's a full-on hurricane!

TIME TRAVEL

Planes traveling from North America to Europe fly faster than those heading in the opposite direction.

Jet streams were first discovered in the 1920s when weather balloons were used to track winds above Mount Fuji, Japan. During World War II, pilots noticed changes in flying speed between North America and Europe.

In the jet stream, planes can be pushed along by winds of over

185mph.

Fast-flowing "rivers of air" called jet streams help to reduce the travel time. They are found where warm, tropical air meets cold polar air, at an altitude of about

33,000ft.

Jet streams flow from west to east due to Earth's rotation.

SLOW GOING

It can take over **1000 years** for ocean water to travel around the world.

MAP KEY:
Surface currents
Deep-water currents

There's a system of ocean currents known as the "global conveyor belt" that carries water on a slow, epic journey across the globe. The waters are moved by winds (at the surface) as well as temperature and salinity differences (at greater depths).

96,000 cubic miles

is the total amount of water moved by the global conveyor belt, which is about one-third of all the water in the oceans.

2hrs, 53 minutes

is the duration of the fastest civilian flight time from New York to London, set by the supersonic airliner Concorde in 1996, reaching speeds of 1348mph—almost twice the speed of sound.

Mount Everest is so high, it sits in a jet stream. Winds at the top can exceed

80mph.

Planes traveling east to west are slowed down, often adding more than 1 hour to the journey.

The 1000-year cycle means that the end of today's "lap" began at the time of King Canute, who reigned in England from 1016 to 1035 and famously (and unsuccessfully) tried to hold back the sea.

3 months

is the time it takes for a drop of water to travel the 2318 mile length of the Mississippi River. The average speed of 1mph is only about a third the speed that people walk.

The speed of the Mississippi depends on the river's width and depth.

Water in wide, deep channels flows faster than in narrow, shallow channels.

SURF'S UP

In the Pacific Ocean, tsunami waves can travel as fast as a jet plane...

80%

of the world's tsunamis occur in the Pacific. They are caused by tremors on the seabed.

Tsunami waves can cross the **11,000 mile** width of the Pacific Ocean in less than **24 hours.**

Tsunami waves move through the whole depth of the ocean.

Pacific Ocean

The average speed of a passenger jet is **500mph.**

The speed of a tsunami wave depends on the depth of the ocean. In the deepest parts of the Pacific, tsunami waves can travel at nearly

600mph.

The distance between waves can be **310—620 miles** and the time between waves can vary from **5 minutes to 2 hours.**

The waves can be **less than 3ft** in height, but as they reach the shore, they slow down and grow. They don't "break" at the shore, like waves generated by the wind, but rush inland.

...but you could walk faster than the slowest waves.

At sea, surface waves created by the wind can travel at less than 5mph.

Slow offshore waves have a short distance between each wave.

300ft

is the distance between the slowest offshore waves. In deep water, the shorter the distance between wind waves, the slower they travel.

600ft

is the distance between the fastest offshore waves. In deep water, the longer the distance between wind waves, the faster they travel. They can reach speeds of up to 60mph.

◄ When waves grow to a size that moves as fast as the wind, they can't get any bigger. The waves you see breaking at a shoreline are a combination of smaller waves that have traveled at different speeds and combined in shallow water.

In shallow water, the speed of a wave depends on the depth. Friction causes wind waves to slow down in the shallows until they break as surf.

SOUTH AMERICA

Antarctica

AUSTRALIA

Some waves circle Antarctica without ever reaching land, while the west coast of North America can experience storm waves that started near New Zealand, right across the Pacific. ►

WIDE OPEN SPACES

Every year, the Sahara grows by more than five times the size of London.

607 sq miles
—the area of Greater London

10%

is the amount that the Sahara has grown since 1920. It is currently expanding at a rate of **2935 sq miles** a year and it now covers **3.6 million sq miles.**

Expansion of the Sahara northwards is caused partly by natural cycles, and partly by climate change as a result of human activity. In 2007, countries in Africa united to plant an **5000 mile** wall of trees across the Sahel to hold back the growing desert. This is known as the Great Green Wall.

Great Green Wall

SHIFTING SANDS

Sand dunes move across a desert, but can be as slow as 16 footsteps a year.

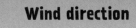 **Wind direction**

The speed of a sand dune depends on its size and the wind speed—as well as any vegetation that may be holding it back. Smaller dunes move faster than larger ones.

15mph

—the wind speed needed to start moving sand across a landscape.

The dunes themselves don't move, but the sand in them is picked up and deposited downwind.

116

h   a   r   a

100 million years ago,

the Sahara was a lush, fertile land home to numerous meat-eating dinosaurs and reptiles, including *Spinosaurus* —the largest known land predator.

The desert is expanding more quickly in the south, where it meets a semi-dry region called the Sahel.

Sahel

Lake Chad

I   C   A

The volume of Lake Chad in the Sahel is a good indicator of conditions, having shrunk since the 1960s by

90%.

Dune movement

330ft

—the annual distance that crescent-shaped sand dunes in northern China moved in the 1950s.

Sand dunes have also been found in Space: on Venus, Mars, and on Saturn's moon Titan. Those on Venus resemble ones on Earth's seabed. They probably formed in a similar way, as the planet's atmosphere is thick and waterlike.

SLIPPERY SLOPE

The sloping ground beneath our feet is very gradually moving all the time...

The movement, known as soil creep, is caused by burrowing animals, the wetting and drying (and freezing and thawing) of the soil, and the pull of gravity.

Most movement occurs near the surface, in the top 10 inches of soil.

1 inch

is the amount of ground movement in a year on some slopes. We can't feel it, but we can see the effects around us, as trees, fences, and posts begin to tilt on hillsides and cracks appear in roads.

Curves in tree trunks are a sign of creep—the tree's base has moved downslope, but not the deeper roots, which tilts the trunk.

The roots of plants and shrubs can help to prevent creep. Terraces (horizontal levels) can also be built on a hillside to slow the movement.

Soil creep is most common when moist soil particles slip past each other. Wet soil swells and then contracts as it dries, causing the soil to move slowly down a slope.

...but sometimes the land can move faster than an Olympic sprinter.

30–50mph

is the speed that most landslides travel at. They're usually caused when soil or mud becomes water-logged and heavy after excessive rain or snow, but they can also be triggered by earthquakes and volcanoes.

In 1980, the eruption of Mount St. Helens in the USA caused the world's largest landslide of modern times. **0.7 cubic miles** of rock and soil fell from the mountain, travelling about 14 miles at speeds more than five times faster than an Olympic sprinter, or up to

150mph.

One of the largest landslides we can still see evidence of today was caused by an earthquake in Iran 10,000 years ago. **4.8 cubic mi.** of soil and rock fell and traveled more than 8.5 miles across the valley floor, damming the Karkheh River.

27.3mph
—top speed of the world's fastest man, Usain Bolt

HOT STUFF

Flowing lava can race almost as fast as a greyhound...

43mph
—the top speed of a greyhound

40–60mph

1830°F
—the scorching temperature of the lava as it raced down the mountain's steep slope.

was the speed of the world's fastest lava flow. It was recorded in 1977 at Mount Nyiragongo, in the Democratic Republic of the Congo. The eruption spewed an unusual type of lava that was almost as thin as water.

Mount Nyiragongo is **11,385ft** high and its magma chamber is about **10mi** beneath Earth's surface.

4.8 sq miles

was the area covered by the lava flow, smothering a **6mi** stretch of road in the process.

The name "lava" comes from the Italian word "lavare," for "stream."

80%

of Earth's surface is covered in cooled lava. The rest is formed of sedimentary and metamorphic rocks.

If the lava is sticky and flowing across a flat surface, rather than through a channel or tube, it can move at less than

1mph.

In 1950, the lava erupting from Mauna Loa, a volcano in Hawaii was traveling at 5.5mph—about a fast walking pace.

There are 4 different types of lava:

pahoehoe, aa, pillow, and blocky.

Pahoehoe is smooth, aa is rocky, pillow forms mounds underwater, and blocky is the slowest-flowing type. Blocky lava gradually forms big boulders which can be over 330ft tall, but usually topple over.

The more silica there is in lava, the stickier it is and the slower it flows. Thick lava usually cools and hardens before it travels very far.

Cooled lava also covers **90%** of the surface of Venus and **50%** of Mars.

SHOCK WAVES

The largest earthquake ever recorded traveled 100 times faster than a cheetah...

78mph
—the top speed of a cheetah

South America

C H I L E

Earthquakes are measured using a magnitude scale. The measurement depends on the length of the fault where the quake occurs. A magnitude of 12 would need a fault larger than Earth itself. The Chilean earthquake was **600 miles long.**

In 1960, a huge earthquake hit Chile traveling at

7830mph.

1960 Chilean Earthquake

Chile's was the strongest earthquake ever recorded—a "megaquake" with a magnitude of

9.5.

The earthquake killed over **1600 people** and left around **2 million** people homeless.

1 million earth tremors occur every year around the world—that's about 300 a day, but most are too small to be felt

...but the world's slowest earthquake lasted 32 years and traveled about 0.4 inches a year —less than the width of a finger.

0.4in ↕

▼ Most earthquakes are over in a matter of minutes, but some can rumble on for months or even years. In 2021, a study of coral colonies in Sumatra, Indonesia, found evidence of a slow-slip earthquake that had lasted from 1829 to 1861.

SUMATRA

0.04–0.08in.

◀ is the rate that scientists found the coral had been sinking every year. However, this increased up to **0.4in. a year** from 1829.

↓ **0.4 inches**

In 1861, this slow movement ended with a devastating earthquake, with a magnitude of

8.5.

Indonesia

The 1861 earthquake triggered a massive tsunami in which thousands of people lost their lives.

Scientists hope that evidence of slow-slip quakes can be used to help to predict larger quakes before they happen.

SPINNING AROUND

We're flying through space at over 1.2 million mph.

The length of Earth's orbit around the Sun is **584 million mi.**

For Earth to travel this distance in a year requires speeds of about

67,000mph.

Los Angeles

New York

This means we travel a distance equivalent to the width of the USA (from Los Angeles to New York) and back again every **5 minutes.**

TIME TO GROW

The days are getting longer.

Scientists think Earth's rotation is slowing down because of the Moon's gravitational pull. As Earth slows down, the Moon slowly moves away. Scientists think that over the past 1.4 billion years, the Moon has moved away from Earth by 27,340 miles.

Over **3** billion years ago,

Earth's day was around six hours long. As the days lengthened, the only living organisms—single -celled microbes—began producing oxygen, eventually creating enough oxygen to make complex life forms possible.

124

Earth's daily rotation is also fast! As if traveling on a spinning ball, people at the poles are moving very little, while those at the Equator are moving at about

1000mph.

Space rockets are often launched close to the Equator because the faster spin gives them a bigger boost, increasing their speed.

Scientists believe that our Solar System is drifting along at about 43,000mph compared to the motion of nearby star systems. But it is also orbiting the center of the Milky Way at about

515,000mph.

But our galaxy, the Milky Way, is also moving. Scientists estimate the Milky Way is flying through space at

1.2 million mph.

1.4 billion years ago,

Earth's day was about 18 hours long.

70 million years ago,

days were half an hour shorter than they are today.

Right now we're gaining about 1.8 milliseconds a century.

00:00:0018

GLOSSARY

acidic Something that contains an acid and has a low pH level. Powerful acids can erode and eat away other substances.

altitude The height of an object in relation to sea level or ground level.

arable Land that is suitable for growing crops.

arid Very dry, due to little or no rain.

asteroid A small rocky object that orbits the Sun.

atmosphere The layers of gases that surround a planet.

atmospheric pressure The pressure exerted by the weight of the atmosphere.

circumference The distance around a circle or other curved figure.

climate change A change in long-term weather patterns and temperatures.

colony A group of living things of the same type that live together.

condense To change from a gas to a liquid or solid.

continent A major landmass on Earth, which is mainly surrounded by sea.

dense When something is closely compacted.

dissolve When a solid becomes incorporated into a liquid to form a solution.

dormant Temporarily inactive, such as a volcano.

elevation The height above a given level.

Equator An imaginary line around Earth's middle which divides Earth into the northern and southern hemispheres.

erosion When something is worn away, by wind or water, for example.

evaporation The process of turning from a liquid into a gas.

extinction When a species dies out.

friction A force that resists the movement of objects or surfaces rubbing together.

glacier A large body of slow-moving ice that forms on land.

global warming The long-term increase in Earth's average temperatures, due to human activities.

gravity The force by which a planet or other body attracts objects toward its center.

hemoglobin A protein in blood that transports oxygen.

humid When there are high levels of water vapor in the air.

indigenous Originating from a particular place.

inhabitable When a place is suitable to live in.

magnetic field The region around a magnetic material, where magnetic forces act.

meteoroids Space rocks. If meteoroids reach a planet's surface, they're called meteorites, but the friction of a planet's atmosphere can cause them to burn up as meteors or "shooting stars."

molecules Two or more atoms joined together. Molecules are the smallest unit of a chemical compound.

molten Something that's been reduced to liquid form by intense heating and melting.

organism A living thing made up of one or more cells.

phenomenon An event that is observed to happen.

Pliocene Epoch A period in history from about 5.3 million to 2.6 million years ago.

poles The points at the top and bottom of a planet, around which the planet rotates.

radiation Energy that can travel through space as particles or waves.

rotation Movement in a circle around a fixed point.

satellite An object that orbits another larger object. Satellites can be natural or artificial.

seismic waves Waves of energy produced by an earthquake, volcano, or other explosive event.

solidify To become hard or solid.

uninhabitable When a place is not suitable to live in.

INDEX

aluminum 92, 95, 99
Amazon Rainforest 56, 69, 76
Amazon River 68-69
Andes 70-71
Angel Falls 18
Antarctica 33, 34, 37, 47, 57, 110-111
arches, natural 66-67
Arctic Ocean 52
Asia 84, 102-103
Atacama Desert 32-33
Atlantic Ocean 44, 81
atmosphere 8-9
Australia 66-67, 77, 82, 85

Baikal, Lake 74
Bentley Subglacial Trench 20
black smokers 52-53

Canada 26, 65, 75, 78, 86
canyons 64
Caspian Sea 74
caves 24-25
Chad, Lake 56, 117
Challenger Deep 16
Chimborazo, Mount 14-15
coral reefs 72-73
core, Earth's 15, 17, 54-55, 92
craters 22-23
crust, Earth's 17, 92
cyclones 29, 44

Daintree Rainforest 77
Dead Sea 20, 35
Death Valley 33, 46
deserts 32-33, 56-57, 103, 116-117
diameter, Earth's 8, 15

earthquakes 40-41, 49, 55, 119, 122-123
Equator 8, 15, 53, 90, 125
Everest, Mount 11, 12, 15, 16, 113

food production 59, 98-99

geysers 60-61
glaciers 35, 36-37, 38
global warming 38, 63
gold 96-97
gravity 13, 15, 27, 37, 110, 124
Great Barrier Reef 72-73
Greenland 37, 82, 98-99

hailstones 30
hurricanes 44

ice 35, 36-37, 38, 63, 91
ice sheets 37, 39, 57, 82, 110
icebergs 36
Iceland 81, 88-89
Indian Ocean 44, 53

jet streams 112-113

Kármán Line 8
Kola Superdeep Borehole 16

La Réunion 29
lakes 35, 56, 74-75, 86, 117
Lambert Glacier 36
landslides 40, 108, 119
lightning 106

magma/lava 13, 14, 48-49, 50, 51, 58, 120-121
Maldives 20
Malta 87
Manitoulin Island 75
mantle, Earth's 17
Mariana Trench 11, 16
Mars 14-15, 121
Mauna Kea 13
Mawsynram 28
Mediterranean Sea 26-27
metals 17, 54-55, 59, 92, 95, 96-97
Mexico City 81
mid-ocean ridge 52, 70-71
Midnight Sun 63, 89
Moon 10, 22-23, 27, 47, 124
mountains 12-15, 21, 29, 65, 70-71, 91, 108-109

Nanga Parbat 108-109
Nauru 83
Nile, River 68
North and South Poles 41, 88, 91, 125

ocean currents 79, 112-113
ocean depths 11, 16, 42
Oceania 85
oil 94
Olympus Mons 14-15
orbit, Earth's 124-125
oxygen 21, 76, 92, 124

Pacific Ocean 42, 44, 50-51, 52, 80, 114
plate tectonics 43, 48-49, 50, 64, 70-71, 80-81
populations 84-85, 100-105

rainbows 107
rainfall 28-29, 32-33, 46, 87
rainforests 56, 69, 76-77
Ring of Fire 51
rivers 35, 68-69, 113

Sahara Desert 32, 56, 116-117
sand dunes 56, 116-117
Sargasso Sea 79
sea levels, rising 20, 37, 38-39
Sea of Marmara 43
seamounts 13
seas 43
seasons 90-91
snow 57, 98
snowflakes 31
Son Doong Cave 24
space 8, 10, 22-23, 46-47, 61, 117
stalagmites and stalactites 24-25
storms 30, 44-45

Thor, Mount 65
tides 26-27
tsunamis 41, 114, 123
Tugela Falls 19
typhoons 44, 45

Uluru 66-67

Venus 46, 107, 121
Verkhoyansk 62-63
Victoria Falls 19
volcanoes 13, 14, 49, 50-51, 58-59, 71, 75, 119, 120-121
Vulcan Point Island 75

water, fresh 34-35, 62, 87
water, salt 27, 34-35, 42, 52-53, 79
waterfalls 18-19
waves 40-41, 114-115
winds 44, 110-111

Xianren Bridge 66

Yarlung Tsangpo 64

ACKNOWLEDGMENTS

The publishers would like to thank the following sources for their kind permission to reproduce the pictures in this book. The page numbers for each of the photographs are listed below, giving the page on which they appear in the book and any location indicator (c-center, t-top, b-bottom, l-left, r-right).

Cover front tl shutterstock.com/Nina Van Pan, tc shutterstock.com, tr shutterstock.com, bl shutterstock.com/CHULKOVA NINA, bc shutterstock.com, br shutterstock.com, spine shutterstock.com/Art Alex, back tr shutterstock.com/Festa, Olha1981 and matrioshka, bl shutterstock.com/ActiveLines and Veronika108, 1cb shutterstock.com/Art Alex, 2-3 shutterstock.com/ActiveLines and SaveJungle, 3r shutterstock.com/Save nature and wildlife, 4t shutterstock.com/Sandinashr, 4bl shutterstock.com/VectorMine, 4br shutterstock.com/Designua, 5tr shutterstock.com/Fast_Cyclone, 8cr shutterstock.com/Inkoly, 8-9c shutterstock.com/Art Alex, 9 shutterstock.com/Macrovector, 10tr shutterstock.com/Sira Anamwong, 12b, 16c, 18c shutterstock.com/Nina Van Pan, 14-15 shutterstock.com/Intrepix, 15br shutterstock.com/Invision Frame, 17 shutterstock.com/CHULKOVA NINA, 19bc shutterstock.com/Kindlena, b shutterstock.com/Zoltan Major, 20 shutterstock.com/d1sk, tl shutterstock.com/bomg, tr shutterstock.com/SkyPics Studio, 21tr shutterstock.com/parose, bl shutterstock.com/NotionPic, 22tl, 23tr shutterstock.com/Pogorelova Olga, 22b courtesy of NASA, 24l, 26tl shutterstock.com/burbura, 24bc, 25c shutterstock.com/Macrovector, 25c shutterstock.com/Zakharchenko Anna, 26tr shutterstock.com/Amanita Silvicora, 26l shutterstock.com/Yauhen 44, 26-27b shutterstock.com/Peter Hermes Furian, 27tc shutterstock.com/Art Alex, 27br shutterstock.com/RNko7, 28t shutterstock.com/Dimokstok, 29t shutterstock.com/LineTale, b shutterstock.com/Creative Commons, 30br shutterstock.com/Rvector, 31 shutterstock.com/paranormal, 32-33 shutterstock.com/SaveJungle, 32t shutterstock.com/Kitigan, 32-33b shutterstock.com/Fast_Cyclone, 34c shutterstock.com/Art Alex, 34b Creative Commons, 35t shutterstock.com/SaveJungle, 35b shutterstock.com/dodoit, 36-37t shutterstock.com/Festa, 36r shutterstock.com/ivector, 36br Creative Commons, 37tl Creative Commons, 37b shutterstock.com/curiosity, 38-39t shutterstock.com/Sky and glass, 39t shutterstock.com/Steinar, 38-39b shutterstock.com/AnnstasAg, 39br Creative Commons, 40-41 shutterstock.com/AlexanderTrou, 40tr shutterstock.com/artestudio, 40c shutterstock.com/Panda Vector, 40b shutterstock.com/Mind Pixell, 41tr shutterstock.com/AlinArt, 41c Creative Commons, 41bl shutterstock.com/Macrovector, 42 Creative Commons, 42br shutterstock.com/Macrovector, 43 Creative Commons, 45 Creative Commons, 45cr shutterstock.com/Modvector, 45br shutterstock.com/jeffhobrath, 46t shutterstock.com/patrimonio designs ltd, 46b shutterstock.com/Art Alex, 47t shutterstock.com/Festa, 48? shutterstock.com/matrioshka, 47cb shutterstock.com/Olha1981, 47b shutterstock.com/Art Alex, 48-49 shutterstock.com/Designua, 49t shutterstock.com/Vasi-lyeva Larisa, 49b shutterstock.com/Ekaterina_Mikhaylova, 50bl shutterstock.com/ivector, 51t shutterstock.com/tunasalmon, 51br shutterstock.com/Ekaterina_Mikhaylova, 52-53t shutterstock.com/VikiVector, 53t shutterstock.com/Viktoriia Protsak, 53bl shutterstock.com/K-K Vectors, 53b shutterstock.com/Ekaterina_Mikhaylova, 54tl shutterstock.com/Art Alex, 54-55 shutterstock.com/CHULKOVA NINA, 54b shutterstock.com/Art Alex, 55c shutterstock.com/Art Alex, 55c shutterstock.com/Designua, 56c shutterstock.com/Spreadthesign, 56l shutterstock.com/VectorMine, 56r shutterstock.com/NotionPic, 56b Creative Commons, 57t shutterstock.com/Festa, 56b shutterstock.com/Lemberg Vector studio, 58b shutterstock.com/Porcupen, 59t shutterstock.com/Ekaterina_Mikhaylova, 59c shutterstock.com/Gvardgraph, 59bl shutterstock.com/Oliver Hoffmann, 59bc shutterstock.com/SkyPics Studio, 59br shutterstock.com/Macrovector, 60l shutterstock.com/VECTOR-16, 60c shutterstock.com/TeddyandMia, 61r shutterstock.com/VECTOR-16, 61cr shutterstock.com/MarySan, 61bl shutterstock.com/Art Alex, 61br shutterstock.com/WinWin artlab, 62t shutterstock.com/Viktorija Reuta, 62tl shutterstock.com/KittyVector, 62-63c shutterstock.com/Flat vectors, 62cr shutterstock.com/Mark_Rimsky, 62br shutterstock.com/NYgraphic, 63br shutterstock.com/Zlatko Guzmic, 64t shutterstock.com/Spreadthesign, 64r shutterstock.com/Nina Van Pan, 64l shutterstock.com/osonmez2, 64bl shutterstock.com/SaveJungle, 65r shutterstock.com/lemono, 65l shutterstock.com/Nina Van Pan, 65br shutterstock.com/Mascha Tace, 67tr shutterstock.com/patrimonio designs ltd, 66-67c shutterstock.com/Sandinashr, 66cr shutterstock.com/elena_aldonina, 67cl shutterstock.com/NotionPic, 76cr shutterstock.com/VEC-TOR-16, 68l Creative Commons, 68-69 shutterstock.com/SaveJungle, 69bc shutterstock.com/VectorMine, 70tc shutterstock.com/Cartarium, 70-71t shutterstock.com/MuchMania, 70bl Creative Commons, 71bc shutterstock.com/KittyVector, 72-73 shutterstock.com/rina Voloshina, 71bc shutterstock.com/KittyVector, 72-73 shutterstock.com/Mirifada, 72tl shutterstock.com/vasosh, 72cr shutterstock.com/Designua, 72-73b shutterstock.com/Natali Snailcat, 72-73b shutterstock.com/Natali Snailcat, 73tc shutterstock.com/akkachai thothubthai, 73r shutterstock.com/vector, 74tl shutterstock.com/Maquiladora, 74c shutterstock.com/NotionPic, 74cl shutterstock.com/Mark_Rimsky, 74b shutterstock.com/Ksngawa, 75b shutterstock

com/Rainer Lesniewski, 75br Creative Commons, 76t Creative Commons, 76-77b shutterstock.com/ActiveLines, 76-77b shutterstock.com/SaveJungle, 77tr shutterstock.com/vasosh, 77br shutterstock.com/Save nature and wildlife, 77bl shutterstock.com/thebeststocker, 78tr shutterstock.com/GoodStudio, 78cl shutterstock.com/Eugene Ga, 78cr shutterstock.com/brichuas, 78br Creative Commons, 79 shutterstock.com/WindVector, 79bl shutterstock.com/Evgeniy Kazantsev, 79br shutterstock.com/GoodStudio, 80t Creative Commons, 80-81b shutterstock.com/Lemberg Vector studio, 80bc Creative Commons, 81t Creative Commons, 82t shutterstock.com/Eugene Ga, 82b Creative Commons, 83t Creative Commons, 83c shutterstock.com/Radzas2008, 83bl Creative Commons, 83cr shutterstock.com/Mountain Brothers, 83bc shutterstock.com/haibo li, 84tc shutterstock.com/Volina, 85t shutterstock.com/SaveJungle, 85cl shutterstock.com/Farizun Amrod Saad, 85b Crea-tive Commons, 86 shutterstock.com/SaveJungle, 86tr Creative Commons, 86c shutterstock.com/Yaroslav Shkuro, 86bl shutterstock.com/Bardocz Peter, 86br shutterstock.com/Lilanakani, 87t shutterstock.com/Anastasia Boiko, 87tr shutterstock.com/deeg, 87c shutterstock.com/Vlasov_38RUS, 87cr Creative Commons, 88-89t shutterstock.com/Peter Hermes Furian, 88-89c shutterstock.com/Rimma R, 88-89b shutterstock.com/Art Alex, 90-91t shutterstock.com/Sky and glass, 90-91t shutterstock.com/Malchev, 90cl shutterstock.com/Visual Generation, 90b shutterstock.com/EMJAY SMITH and pandora64, 91bl Creative Commons, 91br Shutterstock.com/Elena Kelman, 92 shutterstock.com/sharpner, 92b shutterstock.com/CHULKOVA NINA, 93t shutterstock.com/Login, 93br shutterstock.com/Malachy666, 94tr shutterstock.com/Nadia Snopek, 94t shutterstock.com/Boro-datch, 94b shutterstock.com/VectorMine, 95t shutterstock.com/Comscreen, 95tr shutterstock.com/Spreadthesign, 95bl shutterstock.com/Colorcocktail, 95br shutterstock.com/Sira Anamwong, 96-97tc shutterstock.com/Paragorn Dangsombroon, 96cl and 97cr shutterstock.com/Sensvector, 96-97b shutterstock.com/Neliakott, 97tr shutterstock.com/GoodStudio, 97cr shutterstock.com/Igogosha, 97br shutterstock.com/AlinArt, 98-99t shutterstock.com/ActiveLines, 98-99c shutterstock.com/Hennadii H, 98-99b shutterstock.com/Embli25, 98bc shutterstock.com/Tartila, 99tr shutterstock.com/Victoria Sergeeva and Panda Vector, 99cl shutterstock.com/Modvector and wowomnom, 99br shutterstock.com/Vo-lina, 100-101 shutterstock.com/Pyty, 102-103 shutterstock.com/Sky and glass, 103t shutterstock.com/okili77, 103b shutterstock.com/alaver, 104-105t shutterstock.com/brichuas and Yoko Design, 104bl Creative Commons, 104bc shutterstock.com/Radzas2008, 105bl shutterstock.com/Bardocz Peter, 105br Creative Commons, 105b shutterstock.com/vanzki, 106 shutterstock.com/GraphicsRF.com, 107t shutterstock.com/ActiveLines, 107bl shutterstock.com/Veronika108, 108tl shutterstock.com/Patrick Poendl, 108-109b shutterstock.com/SaveJungle, 109t shutterstock.com/SaveJungle, 109c shutterstock.com/petovarga, 110-111t shutterstock.com/Konstantin Yolshin and AnnstasAg, 110-111tc Creative Commons, 110-111b shutterstock.com/Designua, 111c shutterstock.com/robuart, 111cr shutterstock.com/Shanvood, 112tl shutterstock.com/rawipad shaiyes, 112tr shutterstock.com/Macrovector, 112-113t shutterstock.com/Dzianis_Rakhuba, 112cr shutterstock.com/Vega_7, 112-113bc shutterstock.com, 113tc shutterstock.com/Equipoise, 113cr shutterstock.com/rawipad shaiyes, 113br shutterstock.com/TeddyandMia, 114 Creative Commons, 114c shutterstock.com/tovovan, 114b shutterstock.com/AlexanderTrou,115c shutterstock.com/Mikhail Bakunovich, 115b Creative Commons, 116tl shutterstock.com/Ink Drop, 116-117t shutterstock.com/WindVector, 117tr shutterstock.com/YUCALORA, 118tl shutterstock.com/judyjump, 118cr shutterstock.com/Eroshka, 118cl shutterstock.com/petovarga, 119 shutterstock.com/VectorPlotnikoff, 120-121t shutterstock.com/LoopAll, 120tl shutterstock.com/Inspiring, 120-121c shutterstock.com/Veleri, 122tl shutterstock.com/Shanvood, 122-123tc shutterstock.com/Olli Turho, 122-123b shutterstock.com/Bro Studio, 123tl shutterstock.com/stas11, 123tr shutterstock.com/wannawit_vck, 123bc shutterstock.com/Peter Hermes Furian, 123br shutterstock.com/Natali Snailcat, 124tc shutterstock.com/Ad_hominem, 125tc shutterstock.com/MicroOne and Art Alex, 125tr shutterstock.com/KittyVector, 125br shutterstock.com/EvGenius98